FOREWORD BY PERRY BELCHER

Clubhouse
Guidebook

The Ultimate Guide To
The New *Invite-Only* Social Media App
That **Everyone's Talking About**

FOREWORD BY PERRY BELCHER

Clubhouse
Guidebook

The Ultimate Guide To
The New *Invite-Only* Social Media App
That **Everyone's Talking About**

MBO^R Productions

DEBORAH COLE, ALICIA LYTTLE
AND ANGIE NORRIS

CLUBHOUSE GUIDEBOOK

The Ultimate Guide To The New Invite-Only Social Media App That Everyone's Talking About
Copyright © 2021 by Deborah Cole, Alicia Lyttle, Angie Norris
First Edition 2021

Library of Congress Cataloging in-Publication Data:
Cole, Deborah; and Lyttle, Alicia; and Norris, Angie
CLUBHOUSE GUIDEBOOK: The Ultimate Guide To The New Invite-Only Social Media App That Everyone's Talking About

ISBN: 978-1-954712-01-0 (Paperback)

ASIN: B08SPY5Q4D (Kindle, eBook)

1. Business & Economics 2. E-Commerce 3. Internet Marketing
Printed and bound in the United States of America

Published By:
MBO ® Productions
1225 Franklin Ave. Ste 32
Garden City, NY 11530-1693
(760) 410-8009
Publishing.LIVE

WAYS YOU CAN KEEP IN TOUCH WITH US
+ A Few Gifts We've Got For You:

Meet The Authors:

CoachDebCole.com
AliciaLyttle.com
AngieNorris.com

Thank you for purchasing Clubhouse Guidebook!
We have a **pile of bonuses** for all our readers.
Go grab 'em here:
ClubhouseGuidebook.com

We want to meet you! We'd love to hear your
favorite tips, hacks and secrets with Clubhouse.
Share your comments and ideas from this book
on our blog.

Be a part of the conversation + our next book!
ClubhouseConversations.com

The Clubhouse Conversations Blog will keep you updated on all the latest Clubhouse updates and exciting changes as the app comes out of beta and is available to the general public. We're also sharing quick, how-to videos, showing you exactly how to use new Clubhouse features on our blog, step-by-step.

Join Us On Facebook & Be A Part Of The Clubhouse Community: To join the fastest-growing, private Facebook group on how to use Clubhouse for your business or brand and get an invite if you want to join us while we're in beta:

Visit Us On Facebook:

ClubhouseConversions.com

Join Us Every Wednesday at 3pm PT / 6pm ET in our NEW Club room:

Podcast Conversations

Our Club in Clubhouse is where we interview special guests who are succeeding with Clubhouse and expanding their brand using social media. We've got an exciting line up of Celebrities, Entrepreneurs and thought-leaders you'll want to meet and learn from.

Be sure to follow the **Podcast Conversations** Club and the Authors of the book to get invited into our private VIP Club rooms.

And if you're not no Clubhouse yet, that's ok, because we found a way to share Clubhouse Tips and Guests with you – on our NEW Podcast where we have permission to record our rooms to share with you.

Subscribe to our NEW Podcast on Spotify:
Clubhouse Conversations

Would you make a great podcast guest on our show?

Please email our Producer with your pitch and bio at:
ClubhouseConversations@gmail.com

FOREWORD:
BY PERRY BELCHER

From the moment I got on Clubhouse, I realized this is a revolutionary app! Might even be the hottest app that we've seen in a long time.

Anyone can be "on stage" with the Clubhouse App.

It has given everyone a voice and a platform to host a room with just five people in it or five hundred.

Now, you get to be the host and drive the show and see if you're good enough to carry it or not.

Clubhouse is the great equalizer; we see where the app is flourishing with women, people of color, and those who were shy before and would never walk up in the front of the room physically to speak to an audience.

It's really an enormous social experiment.

I take tons of notes when I'm listening to great speakers in rooms.

You can track trends and hear how people are thinking or how people are feeling about certain things. Now, I can go on Clubhouse App and predict the temperature of the water depending on what business I might want to invest in.

Clubhouse gives easy access and the ability for anybody to start a room - a room to talk about anything. In fact, many rooms are like the Seinfeld show, "A Show About Nothing." And on a certain level, there'll be an audience for any room that's started. So if you want to get on and talk about building Legos, you can get on and talk about building Legos, which I'm sure they're probably doing right now.

You can talk about business, investing, song-writing, pregnancy, relationships, and divorce or find a support group for whatever interests you.

Clubhouse is going to be very hot for a long time. You can count on that!

TikTok is the new Television, and Clubhouse is a whole new brand of radio.

We're going to see a whole new way of music collaboration using the Clubhouse App.

My son is an accomplished musician, and he's on there with other musicians talking about the future of the music industry and how people will collaborate to create new music.

Soon, they'll figure out devices to plug into Clubhouse and make an album together with musicians from all around the world.

We're going to see an increasing variety of uses for the platform - certainly more than what we see now.

The app is addicting, especially if you love gathering data and learning about people.

When I first got onto Clubhouse and started a room, CoachDeb was moderating for me, and when I had to bounce, I handed over control of the room to her so she could keep it going as long as she liked.

Then she sends me a text saying, "We're going to keep this room going and make it one of the longest-running rooms to date on the app."

I woke up the next morning and hopped back on to the app, and noticed the room w as still going. Guess she was right. People didn't want to leave the room.

You're going to see many opportunities for excellent moderators to have a full-time job being moderators for prominent speakers.

Another revolution that you'll see in the media space with Clubhouse factors in its 24-hour access. Clubhouse app is a media channel, just like television. And the early adopters of the platform will have a considerable advantage over the laggards that think it's just going to be a fad.

Clubhouse is a network in and of itself!

You've got content. You've got channels. That's what the media industry is made of.

If you've got a Club, that's one channel. Then, you can put programming on it. Own a channel or a show, and you can host other people's shows on your channel.

When Clubhouse goes that route, where you'll see more channels pop up that have independent shows within the channel, that's when people will understand the power of the media channel.

For example, I have the Growth Hacking Club - that's a Channel. Now, if I wanted to have CoachDeb's show on my channel, she'd come on at a certain time every week and host her show on my channel.

When my friends ask me what I thought about Clubhouse, I tell them it's a channel that gives you an instant audience.

Will Clubhouse hurt LIVE events in the future?

I believe it'll do the opposite.

I think you'll see people gain confidence from using the app, and they'll realize how fun it is and want to go to events in person to meet the person or guru they've been talking to on Clubhouse.

Live events will suddenly become more interactive. Instead of just having people on stage talking at the audience, they'll find ways to get people more involved, to give more participants a voice.

As for the free advice given on Clubhouse? Well, I think "free advice is worth every penny you had to pay for it."

The great thing about Clubhouse: Clubhouse gives everybody a voice.

The worst thing about Clubhouse: Clubhouse gives everybody a voice.

You've got the wannabe experts on there and the stone-cold experts who've made it in the real world.

On the other hand, the coolest thing about Clubhouse is you have the most prominent tech investors in the world - just hanging out in a room.

One of the biggest, most exciting rooms I've ever been in so far is the virtual dinner party, on Saturday nights, where there were about 4,000 people in the room. This included the influential thought-leaders and entertainers around the world, people with massive audiences and reach. It was quite interesting to hear what's on their minds.

Clubhouse is where everybody is right now. Facebook has lost a lot of its allure. Eyeballs went to earballs on Clubhouse.

I often spent 30 minutes on Facebook; now, I spend almost NO time on Instagram, and I spend forever on Clubhouse every day.

The authors of Clubhouse Guidebook are my friends, and I know these ladies will help you get a massive edge by helping you shortcut the learning curve and teach you how to do Clubhouse right, so you'll gain real influence and genuine fans who will follow you to the ends of the earth.

CoachDeb is one of those influencers I call first anytime I want to know what's going on with social media. I've been calling on her to put her on the largest stages since she wrote the first book on Twitter, back in 2008.

Deb Cole is the person I talk to anytime I've got a question. She's put together this Guidebook with two other online business experts who have made big things happen in the real world of business; Alicia Lyttle and Angie Norris.

You're going to learn all the hacks and tips from these three ladies. Follow and listen to them on Clubhouse. You'll probably hear me in their rooms sharing more of my thoughts... if you like the growth hacking things that I like to talk about.

There are Clubhouse rules, that if violated, will get you ostracized. These ladies will teach you how to be popular without being a prick.

Perry Belcher
CH: @PerryBelcher
Host of The Club Room:
Growth Hacking Club

Join Perry's Monday Morning Meeting for Entrepreneurs. It's like the Virtual Dinner Party - except it's a Virtual Coffee Clutch where you get to eavesdrop on what other top business owners and investors are up to.

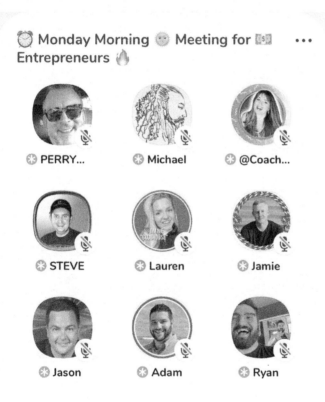

PREDICTIONS FROM @COACHDEB ON CLUBHOUSE

Introducing CoachDeb's 3rd book on "the Next BIG Thing" in Social Media Marketing, since Twitter Revolution was published in 2008.

12 years later...

Since writing Twitter Revolution - the first book published on Twitter, back in 2008, I predicted that it would be the hottest app that would grow into the mainstream. This meant celebrities and, yeah, even presidents using it, and everyone laughed at these predictions of mine. Since then, I haven't been

jazzed enough about the thousands and thousands of other social media platforms that have come and gone and come and grown.

Until now.

August 2020:

I begin writing the book on Clubhouse, sharing chapters exclusively with clients who get on the app before the frenzy begins.

The First Movers get it. The savvy marketers understand its power.

But the app is yet to get in the hands of the top digital marketers until December 10, 2020, when Perry Belcher joins the app and from that moment, an avalanche of other marketers begin to join. People start to get five invites at once, instead of the stingy "only 1 invite" given to new members when the app first started.

The viral spread of invitations begins in the marketing community, and the hottest social media app takes off!

Now that all the digital marketers are joining Clubhouse, I expect the platform to be even more exciting and awesome! The application of Clubhouse rooms and Clubs has only just begun.

Clubhouse 2022 will look dramatically different than Clubhouse 2020.

And we'll be keeping our friends and clients up to date on our blog & podcast with the latest Clubhouse applications and how they can be used for business and brand building. Join us and join the conversation:

ClubhouseConversations.com

DON'T SKATE TO WHERE THE PUCK IS.
SKATE TO WHERE THE PUCK IS GOING.

~ WAYNE GRETZKY

VIRTUAL DINNER PARTIES ... ON CLUBHOUSE

One of my favorite rooms in Clubhouse that I've been participating in every Saturday evening since the Summer of 2020, when all in-person events were shut down, is the Virtual Dinner Parties hosted by Felicia Horowitz.

Each time I join in to listen in has been eye-opening, and quite frankly, an entertaining social outlet during a time when social distancing was the most overused phrase around the world.

Connecting with such innovative minds, thought leaders in tech, and all the Silicon Early Adopters who got an exclusive, early invite to Clubhouse, before it was ever even offered in the App Store in October 2020, has been a true honor.

When my clients and friends ask me why I predict Clubhouse to be the next best thing in social media, I have a few answers that I share with them that I'll share with you here.

First, one of the things that make Clubhouse unique from all the other shiny social media platforms is that it's an audio-only platform.

Audio brings about a different level of empathy that written text doesn't parlay as you see with all the fights on Twitter.

It's been interesting to see movements started as a result of things discussed in Clubhouse, and people working towards solutions in 2020.

Now that more and more marketing minds are joining in, I expect it to be radically different than when it first started. And I like that. It'll evolve, just like Twitter did. And eventually, it may be a place where heated discussions will take place now that a more diverse group of thinkers are on the platform - just like Twitter and Facebook did.

But, whatever Clubhouse becomes years from now, it will be THE place to be in 2021 #HandsDown #MarkMyWords

That's why I'm taking the time out to write this book for you. So you can take advantage of it while it's still in the early adoption phase.

It'll be THE Party, the After Party, The Conference, and the water cooler that people are longing for.

Clubhouse will be the new podcast platform where you'll have to be IN the room when it happens - or else... you'll miss out.

There are no recordings.
There are no replays.
You need to be in the room where it happens.
Or you WILL Miss out.

"IF YOU ARE WORKING ON SOMETHING
EXCITING THAT YOU REALLY CARE
ABOUT,
YOU DON'T HAVE TO BE PUSHED.
THE VISION PULLS YOU.
~ Steve Jobs

FOMO = FEAR OF MISSING OUT

It's a real thing. FOMO might be one of the most powerful psychological motivators in a marketer's toolkit. If you know how to use it strategically, you'll have the hottest selling product or service compared to your competitors.

Clubhouse figured FOMO out like a Champ! The desire to get an invitation to Clubhouse is seen everywhere, all over the other social media platforms, people begging for an invite. People are selling their invites for $4K, $5K, $5,355, and a whopping $7,500!

(BTW: Please do NOT buy an invite to Clubhouse. My co-authors and I have been helping our friends, clients, and followers skip the waitlist with our Clubhouse Trains we run on Thursday nights: ClubhouseTrain.com
But more on Clubhouse Trains later.

Back to the Clubhouse waitlist.

People have been waiting 2-3 months to join Clubhouse over the summer of 2020, so if you're now waiting 2-3 days and getting impatient, imagine the lust for the app that happened while it wasn't even on the app store!

When Clubhouse first came out, invitations were given strategically to Silicon Valley Insiders, Hollywood celebrities and musicians who were among the first to get an exclusive invite to join the app.

Once the app got on the Apple store in October 2020, people began downloading it, just to reserve their name or brand, only to go on the waitlist to join Clubhouse.

Unless you know someone who's already on Clubhouse, and they're willing to share one of their Golden Ticket Invites to you over any other friend of theirs, or you follow our Invite Hack that we shared on one of our first LIVE shows on YouTube, you will be left out in the cold (on the old social media platforms) until you can join Clubhouse.

See how FOMO works so far?

People are relegated to only participate in the old social media apps like Facebook, Instagram and Twitter, places that have almost become barren wastelands compared to the high energy, party popping, club hopping, hot social media app where you can have real conversations by simply hitting your microphone button on your phone and hearing your friend's voice.

Clubhouse Obsessed? Clubhouse Addicted?

Yes, it's happening... to thousands as we speak.

Here's how this works...

Since no recordings take place, FOMO kicks in. You have to be in the room where it happens, so you wind up never leaving a room. That's when the addiction takes over. People are in rooms all night. Falling asleep to Clubhouse is a common habit these days.

I can see the future where people begin going to in-person events again, with their hair covering their right ear, to hide their apple airpod. Why? They're in a Clubhouse room at the same time that they're walking around hallways of conferences or in boring keynote presentations where there is no chance they'll get "invited on stage" as they could on Clubhouse.

Clubhouse will also be the place where comedians, musicians, and artists gather their fans to share their talent.

With this mix of talent, art, entertainment, knowledge, training rooms, and chat rooms, it'll be the place everyone will be talking about and yes, unfortunately, just as I predicted about Twitter in its inception, one day politicians will join in, and use it as their platform to reach and influence the masses.

Consider yourself warned.

And enjoy Clubhouse during its early days... the time when every social media platform is at its best.

In the meantime - I'm looking forward to masterminding with all my marketing friends on the audio-only platform in 2021 and beyond. See you on the platform! Let's SHARE and connect like never before.

But most importantly, let's connect and make something beautiful - as a result of being on the platform.

You can follow me
@CoachDeb,
and let's chat!
Deborah Cole

P.S.: Also, be sure to follow my co-authors and business besties who helped bring this Clubhouse Book to market - FAST.

@ AliciaLyttle
@ AngieNorris

Thank you for reading and sharing Clubhouse Guidebook. This is the 3rd book in my social media predictions trilogy.

I'm excited to share "The Next BIG Thing" on social media with you now, with my co-authors, Alicia & Angie. They have truly become my business besties. And I imagine they'll become yours too... as you turn the virtual pages in your kindle or real, live book you hold in your hands.

Oh! And be sure to let me know which version you got because we've got a pile of bonuses for our readers who've supported us in our writing / blogging / podcasting journey. You'll find those bonuses as you read this book. (Yup, sending you on a little hunt.)

Now I'm looking to hear from you on our NEW Blog: ClubhouseConversations.com where we get to meet you and keep in touch, and hear YOUR Best Clubhouse Tips, Hacks & Strategies in using the app for your business, brand or service.

Happy Clubbin'!

DEDICATION OF THE CLUBHOUSE BOOK: JEREMIAH OWYANG

August 2020

From Coach Deb Cole:

My absolute favorite new addiction... Clubhouse!

When in-person events are postponed, canceled, and held on Zoom instead, we find our souls missing human connection like never before.

Until Clubhouse was born to fill the void.

Every morning, I meet awesome new people from around the world, hear from different perspectives and learn new things about what our future will look like in the world of tech, the music industry, entertainment, wellness, etc.

Thanks, Jeremiah Owyang, for inviting me into Clubhouse over the Summer of 2020, and giving me the best onboarding session to make me feel welcome, and understand the culture and the etiquette of this incredible community.

You've created a #ClubhouseObsessed member in a matter of one week! Connecting with you and the Silicon Valley thought-leaders, hearing what our future will look like, participating in your Wellness Club on Mondays, and joining you for the Saturday night Virtual Dinner Parties have been the highlight of my summer.

Not to mention, hearing from LL Cool J, MC Hammer, and Terry Crews just hang out and talk about current issues of our time! What a treat to be a part of last summer.

My brain is on stimulation overload every time I open the app. Loving Clubhouse! Thank You!

Follow Jeremiah on Clubhouse CH: @Jowyang

Subscribe to Jeremiah's Blog to learn more about how social audio apps are changing the world of business:

Web-Strategist.com/blog

"SOCIAL AUDIO IS THE "GOLDILOCKS MEDIUM", TEXT SOCIAL NETWORKS ARE NOT ENOUGH, VIDEO CONFERENCING IS TOO MUCH, SOCIAL AUDIO IS JUST RIGHT."

~ JEREMIAH, OWYANG

Highly recommend you read Jeremiah's recent report: *The Future of Social Audio: Startups, Roadmap, Business Models, and a Forecast.*

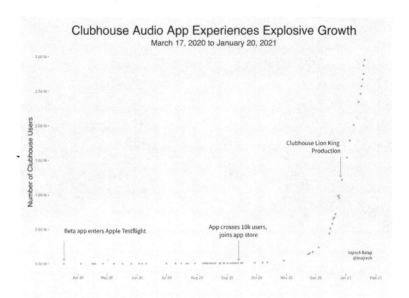

Above Graphic: Clubhouse Social Audio Platform (I joined in June 2020) has shown explosive hockey stick growth, starting with a small group in beta, hitting the 10k mark and joining the Apple App store, witnessing the Lion King performances, and growing in international markets.

Data from technology and economics expert Vajresh Balaji. Follow Vajresh on Twitter for more analytics on Clubhouse and tech: @bvajresh but only if you want to get way smarter.

TABLE OF CONTENTS

YOUR CLUBHOUSE CONVERSATIONS + CONNECTIONS +
CLUBS + NOTES   203

CHAPTER 1:
AUDIO IS THE FUTURE

The proliferation of podcasts and smart speakers over the past six or so years has taught us one thing.

Audio is the next revolution of how we do business and interact on social platforms.

It probably sounds like an unbelievable truth, given that most of us have grown accustomed to screens and consuming information visually.

Without putting too much thought into it, you can probably safely say you spend a considerable portion of your day working at your computer, catching up with friends and icons via social media, and unwinding by flipping through the latest Netflix series.

At some point, it's reasonable to assume that we will tire of screens and yearn for an easier way to consume information and share thoughts.

And we are predicting that audio will be the solution. Shocked?

Come on. It isn't that far-fetched! Audio is already offering us a reprieve to a problem that we are slowly realizing we have. Those of us on the brink of screen fatigue have opted to use our voices to control smart speakers like Siri, Alexa, and Google Assistant to work, research, shop, remind and entertain us. Heck, we even have them controlling our lights, locks, and devices.

At the time of writing this book, Loup Venture estimated that 75% of U.S. households would have smart speakers by the end of 2025. Due to population growth, this represents over 100 million households. Tech giants Apple, Amazon, and Google are continually pouring money into their voice control apps. Maybe because they see something the rest of us are only just beginning to.

Why the shift towards audio?

Millennial consumers have changed user demands to keep pace in an ever-evolving digital world. Speed, convenience, and efficiency are always being optimized and what's faster and more convenient than saying what you want from a product or person?

While smart speakers are the primary way we see voice being used now, it is only the beginning of the integration in our daily lives and businesses. Experts have predicted that nearly every application will use voice technology in some way in the next five years.

Voice has established itself as the ultimate user experience as consumers become increasingly comfortable and dependent on using voice to talk to their devices. Particularly, Gen Z will become a digital-native population that knows and demands advanced technologies in their everyday lives - from booking an appointment to applying for jobs.

To maintain their relevance, businesses will need to keep up with their expectations and do two things: integrate audio technology in their business processes and go where the consumers are...on audio-based applications that are fulfilling the population's social needs.

Customized experiences

Smart speakers will continue to offer more personalized experiences as they get better at recognizing different voices. Currently, Google Home can accommodate up to six user accounts and detect unique voices, allowing Google Home users to customize a variety of features.

In only a few years, audio will integrate with everything we do daily, from education to entertainment. We will be able to personalize our experiences as marketers lean more towards niche/individual targeting.

Who else is investing heavily in audio?

Publishers like Richard Lennon of Penguin Audio. According to him, audiobooks' booming popularity corresponds with the rise of podcasts, heralding an age of unquenchable thirst for audio content.

But nowhere is audio seemingly more needed than in the 280-character space of the Twitter universe. Initially crowned as the place to quickly gain and impart ideas and express thoughts to a large audience, it has descended into misconstrued conversations that have led to repeated diatribes against its users by its users.

And the platform's shortfalls haven't gone unnoticed. Just this year, Twitter announced that it wanted to add a more human touch to the way we use Twitter - **your very own voice**.

So, users are now able to tweet up to **140 seconds of audio**. We can only hope the constant barrage of shouting matches disguised as threads will become less if not cease altogether with the ability to hear the true intended meanings of ideas and expressions in context.

It has been reported too that the CEO of Twitter, Jack Dorsey has scouted the hot new audio-based app, Clubhouse. On the heels of his platform's latest feature, it would be remiss of us not to think that our predictions for the future are closer than we imagined.

Clubhouse will become the go-to app for movers, shakers, strategists, influencers, content-providers, and consumers. The ability to share ideas and interests in real-time with a guaranteed response is remarkable! This is what we have been waiting for.

Like smart speakers, the AI on Clubhouse is constantly learning the intricacies that make each member unique and personalize each experience. So users aren't shown random rooms or thrown into incompatible relationships. As you continue to use the app, it learns more about your interests, and what you like, then it curates an experience that is to your unique liking. Could you want a better app?

The only mistake you can make with Clubhouse is not getting in NOW. It's currently the most happening party, the most-talked-about event, the best-attended soiree. Hopping into a room is like walking into a friend's party with all your friends there plus a celebrity or two. You can even pull someone aside and 're-room' for a private conversation.

Forget the arguments on Twitter, the fleeting joys of Facebook, the dance moves you can't seem to catch on TikTok. Enter a room on Clubhouse where minds are meeting and people are actually talking with each other, ebbing and flowing like we're supposed to as social beings.

Get on and get in. Don't wait to perfect a concept or an idea. Conversations on Clubhouse are real and raw with no record. There's no need to have all the i's dotted and t's crossed. That's what makes it so unique. You get to flesh out your ideas right there in a room with hundreds or thousands of ideators throwing some great value your way.

Pandemic proof

With covid-19 causing us to cancel events, seminars, and even house calls, social media has had to fill the gap for social gatherings. Either we spend our nights re-watching everything on Netflix (eye roll), or we head over to Twitter to see what people are up to. Fear of missing out has become a staple during this pandemic. It's probably why the Clubhouse gatherings have included some of the biggest names in Hollywood, sports, academia, tech, and marketing. And they have fallen in love.

In fact, after Kevin Hart, Drake, and Tiffany Haddish had a chat on the app, Hart took to Twitter to announce:

> *"Had an amazing conversation in the Clubhouse app today...Real talks with real people...this is the direction that social media is now going to.*
>
> *Pretty dope."*

Virtual events have moved to Clubhouse.

The go-to seminars with the best speakers giving precious information are all rushing to this FREE platform.

Rooms have boasted the best and brightest minds one only imagined talking to some years ago (think Harlem mogul Diddy and Fox Soul's Jason Lee). Now, they are up close, personal, and willing to talk to rooms of 200-2000 people every day or night!

Clubhouse has become the digital event that never ends, and everyone wants a seat at the table.

The best part?

You don't have to prepare content in advance for Clubhouse. Create as you converse and then use the information garnered on Clubhouse on your other social media platforms. Guide your followers to these platforms and watch your follower count grow exponentially.

We have been members of Clubhouse since early inception and have gained invaluable insights into its inner workings. This book will guide you through the platform and help you make your Clubhouse experience a worthwhile one. Of course, like any app worth its fans, there will be updates, and like any good coach, we will revise this book to include them all, so you're always in the know.

Although the righteous age of radio may never return, Clubhouse is the closest we now have to engage in real-time with real voices to real people. **Here's to the re-emergence of audio!**

IT'S ALMOST AS IF WE ARE GOING BACK... TO THE FUTURE.
@COACHDEB

CHAPTER 2:
NO LIPSTICK REQUIRED

A constant supply of filters, photo-shopped images, and video-based platforms like Zoom and TikTok have left few of us immune to experiencing a lack of body confidence.

And don't go thinking it's just a female issue.

In an online survey of more than 12,000 adults, 6% of men said they were "very to extremely dissatisfied" with their appearance.

Owing to this, many of us have become disenchanted with platforms that require us to pay close attention to our appearance.

Video-based apps have excluded most of us who would rather not dress up every day or even comb our hair and wake up wishing that red pimple on the tip of our nose would hurriedly slip away.

What a colossal relief that we have no such concerns with Clubhouse! Users have participated in rooms while cooking, lounging by the pool, going on runs, and even showering. Cue your week-old stubble or bed head. No one cares because no one will know.

We don't even have to feign interest! Simply hop into a room that interests you and exit if it doesn't live up to your expectations. Speak when you want, listen when you don't. There's no pressure to participate. When you are comfortable enough, host your own room with the topics that drive you and watch the platform bring the audience to you!

Clubhouse is also the most inclusive app of this generation. The hallway belongs to everyone! Anyone can be invited and find a strong representation of their tribe there.

We are particularly pleased that members of the disability community will find entry to this platform has only a few barriers, and the founders are actively working on making the app more accessible once it opens up out of beta and to the public.

(OK, yes, we know Android users are still waiting, but we hear that the creators are working feverishly to make it available soon).

Vaccines are now being distributed to combat the spread of this dreaded virus. Still, until we are allowed to move unrestricted again, Clubhouse is the invite you'll be dying to get on a Saturday night.

NEVER DOUBT THAT A SMALL GROUP OF THOUGHTFUL, COMMITTED CITIZENS CAN CHANGE THE WORLD; INDEED, IT'S THE ONLY THING THAT EVER HAS.

MARGARET MEAD

CHAPTER 3:
COOL NEW WAY TO SHOP & SELL

The Clubhouse app is certainly not a village square to peddle your wares, BUT we have seen some pretty creative strategists build awareness around their brand, which has led to multi-figure sales.

They have made Clubhouse the cool new way to shop... and sell. Members have started to use text messaging to handle sale queries (we go in-depth a bit further in the book).

How?

By funneling the conversations OFF Clubhouse. Now, we know what this may sound like, but it's not what you think. Or maybe it is if you think that the magic continues on other platforms.

Let's explain.

After a member drops valuable nuggets of information or tips in a Clubhouse room that leaves you wanting more (excellent sales tactic), you'll naturally go looking for their profile to learn more about them.

In that profile, you'll come across emojis, words, or hashtags that you are required to text based on the product or service you want. When you do, you'll receive a response with a picture of whatever you wish to purchase and a link where you can make the purchase.

It's absolute genius!

If you have a retail store or offer services but you're not on Clubhouse - you've already lost a considerable chunk of your market.

You'd best believe that your competitors are there, popping in rooms and commanding the attention of potential customers with valuable tips that create an appetite for more. Brick and mortar stores have transformed into click and order establishments.

You should know that the only clickable links on Clubhouse are your Instagram and Twitter accounts. (For now.)

You can leverage these to earn hundreds of followers each time you enter or moderate a room. It may be as

14

simple as asking all room members to send you a DM or follow all the moderators before asking a question.

Once you begin to acquire leads through these accounts, you can start the relationship of converting them to paying customers.

CHAPTER 4:
CLUBHOUSE: ARE YOU MISSING OUT?

Clubhouse...

"OMG! How do I get an invite to Clubhouse?"

This question might be the most asked right now on every other social platform. That, and...

"What IS Clubhouse?"

Serious FOMO is happening online, and it's reaching epic proportions. All because of the hottest new social media app that everybody wants because nobody can join unless they get invited.

We're going to go out on a limb and say that there's probably no one currently on social media who hasn't heard of this new, highly exclusive, secret social media platform that has become the preferred hangout spot for professionals, celebrities, influencers, and tech giants.

This latest Silicon Valley social magnet has turned social media on its head, leaving those in the know with a gripping need to get in on the action.

And that's probably part of the reason you're here! (Yes, we understand that severe FOMO feeling).

The good news is, we have been on the platform since the Summer of 2020 - testing, learning, talking to celebrities, and influencers. We have discovered some down and dirty tips that will help you and your brand stand out on Clubhouse as well as establish authority and convert participants into paying customers.

We must admit that we are all now Clubhouse addicts with an unhealthy appetite for the awesome information shared. However, you'll understand that once you join the platform, there's no going back to regularly scrolling through Twitter or Facebook to pass the time.

It's part of the reason we created this book. Clubhouse has become so much more than an app to us. It is our community - our safe space where our voices can be heard by friends, movers, and shakers without judgment or fear.

We just couldn't keep this great secret to ourselves, and because the App is new (like still in beta stage new), we know that you will have a ton of questions. Throughout this book, we have included tips and hacks (Club Tips) to help you have the best experience on Clubhouse and make your mark while you're there.

Don't forget to join the exclusive Facebook group *"Clubhouse Conversions"* where we give you even more tips on making the most of your Clubhouse experience.

This domain is the shortcut that'll bring you directly to our private Facebook group:

ClubhouseConversions.com

Ok now, are you ready to dive into the best hacks and secrets to succeed on Clubhouse?

Let's start with the most common question on everyone's lips.

CHAPTER 5:
WHAT THE HECK IS CLUBHOUSE?

Clubhouse is a super-exclusive, audio-only app that allows users to hop into themed chat rooms and have one-on-one constructive conversations with others who have common interests, stories, and passions.

It was created by co-founders Paul Davison and Rohan Seth and launched on March 17, 2020.

Members can network, test ideas or if they choose, just listen in on conversations with experts or once inaccessible celebrities, like Oprah Winfrey, Ashton Kutcher, and Kevin Hart. The only equipment needed is your phone and your voice (goodbye overused typing thumb).

The exclusivity of the app is what really sets it apart from other social platforms. The app is not yet public and is currently only available to iPhone users.

Unfortunately, Android users may have to wait until Spring 2021 for access. However, if you have an iPad or iPad mini, you're in luck because you can still get in on the action (yeah!).

After you have downloaded the Clubhouse app from the App Store, the only way to gain access is by invitation from a current user. Invitations are given sparingly, so members usually carefully consider who they allow into this intensely private space. We'll talk about some ways to ensure you get an invitation later on.

Another remarkable feature of the Clubhouse app is the disappearing chat. Conversations are live, and members must be present for every minute of a discussion.

Once a chat room is closed, there is no record of the conversation. This means talks on Clubhouse are private and protected, similar to a conversation held with someone in a conference.

However, you don't have to be staring at the Clubhouse screen for the duration of a conversation to participate. As long as you don't exit the app, you can still listen in and ask questions or give tips while you engage in other activities like cooking or rearranging your office. There is no video component, so there's no need to worry about how you look.

Users have confessed to participating in Clubhouse conversations doing everyday activities like having breakfast and even taking a shower.

At the publication time of this book, 01-21-21 this is what the Clubhouse app icon looked like. A black and white picture of the amazing guitarist Bomani who I met in a small Clubhouse room back in August when you could hang out with him in a small

room of a dozen others just hanging out, enjoying good music, good chat and really good vibes.

Now, you're lucky if his @BomaniX rooms aren't filled up with thousands listening to him play with other song-writers all playing together on the app.

Last month the app icon changed from Bomani to Axel Mansoor who was nominated for an Emmy and hosted hologram concerts. I was in one of the rooms Axel was running, and was so impressed with his ability to connect on such a genuine level while over 1,000 members were in the audience. It was almost like being backstage with him, having an informal conversation with a few new friends who were discovering him for the first time.

As of today, (during this next book update, on the 1 year Birthday of Clubhouse, March 17, 2021) the app icon is about to change again, and showcase another amazing Club member, a woman who contributes value to the app.

Looking forward to meeting @aja_monet who is a poet, actor and Director, in one of the rooms she runs this month.

The app icon changes each month, but you'll want to always look for a black and white picture of a happy person looking off in the distance.

The wrong app is purple and has 2 flag outlines.

BEWARE OF THE PURPLE APP!

The Purple Clubhouse App is NOT the Clubhouse you're looking for.

Android users have reported downloading the Clubhouse app and gaining access to a platform without an invitation. **THAT IS A FAKE APP**. If you are not using an iPhone, iPad, or iPad mini to download the app, you have the wrong app and have not yet joined the real and totally awesome Clubhouse family.

But to answer the question, "What Is Clubhouse?" is a bit like trying to answer "What Is An Event?" because it is something different to every person or group who joins.

For some, it's a place where a small group gathers and connects on their phone to have informal conversations.

To business leaders and speakers, it's a place to gather large audiences to share their knowledge and connect with their audience by bringing them on stage to answer their most pressing questions.

To podcasters, it's a place to interview guests, record the conversation, and repurpose the recording on their podcast, for all of their friends and fans to download and listen to.

For investors, it's a place to allow start-ups to pitch their product or service to them, and find a unicorn to invest in and together be profitable.

The only way to really know "What Is Clubhouse?" is to join the app and participate.

What is Clubhouse to you? Tweet me @CoachDeb and share your favorite use of Clubhouse.

YOUR MIND, ONCE STRETCHED BY A NEW IDEA, NEVER REGAINS ITS ORIGINAL DIMENSIONS.

ADAPTED FROM QUOTE BY:

OLIVER WENDELL HOLMES SR.

CHAPTER 6:
HOW DO YOU JOIN CLUBHOUSE?

By Personal Invitation Only

Remember when we said Clubhouse is an invite-only platform? We weren't kidding. Clubhouse is still in the private beta phase and presently only available to iPhone users. (Sorry Android friends!)

To join Clubhouse, you must be invited by a current member. Each new member is initially allotted one invitation that they can send to someone using their phone numbers.

Participants who are on the platform for a while and frequently engage in conversations and moderate rooms (we'll talk more about this) can earn additional invitations, but this is not guaranteed.

> **Club Tip:**
> To ensure that you receive an invitation from someone on Clubhouse, be ready and willing to offer value and let the person know what you will bring to the platform to help others. Why? Whoever invites you is endorsing your skills and value. Suppose you do something untoward on the platform or offer little or no value to its members. In that case, you may get booted, and the person who nominated or invited you won't be far behind.

The little-known back-door Secret:

Another way of joining Clubhouse is through the lesser-known exclusive back-door.

> **Club Tip:** Find out which of your friends are on Clubhouse and ensure that you are in each other's contacts BEFORE you download Clubhouse.

To use this method, download the app from the App Store and reserve your username. Your friends on Clubhouse who have your phone number will receive a notification that you're waiting for an invite.

Your friends on Clubhouse now have the option to let you in without losing their allotted invitation(s). This is what the notification to them looks like:

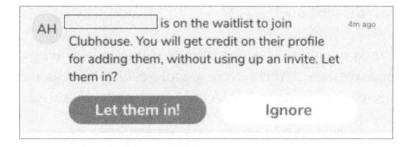

This doesn't always work, but when it does, it's a treat!

A super-secret hack:

Our friend Michael Sanchez shared this hack with us that works for him.

Collect numbers and names of people already on Clubhouse. Add it to a Google contacts list. Share that contact list to a friend who will then add it to their phone contacts (import from Google) then sign up. Ta-da! You get nominated and can delete the contact list you imported with one click.

The Clubhouse Train

Another way we get people in is to have a Clubhouse train. What is a Clubhouse train?

Well, in our Private Facebook group, you see how the trains work in action!

Feel free to join by going to ClubhouseTrain.com and join the next one!

When everyone was desperately trying to get invites, and we heard there were people selling invites for insane amounts, we decided to create a private

community of awesome people who connect and pay it forward" in both their wisdom in the group, as well as sharing their invites to get awesome people into the app.

Typically we kick off a train with one invite, and each person who receives an invite to join Clubhouse pays it forward by sharing their invite with the next person on the waiting list.

During the holidays, we would host a train every Thursday where we have people who have an invitation invite others, and we keep the train going all night until everyone is in the club.

For example, if Sue gives her invite to James, then James gives it to Kim, and then Kim gives it to Lorette, and we keep the train going all night long until everyone is in!

This might be the easiest way to get in, but you have to be an iPhone user, and you have to pass your invite to the next member on the train.

One of the best things I've seen from these Holiday Clubhouse Trains we did every Thursday, was watching the community continue the tradition as we got busy with our own clients and couldn't host a Thursday train one week.

Now, members in the Facebook group simply post if they have an invite to share or need an invite, and the train continues… one post at a time.

PROBA TE DIGNUM

A RISING TIDE LIFTS ALL BOATS

31

I really love our community! Filled with positive, encouraging people, all willing to help one another succeed.

William Tong, is a perfect example of the spirit of Clubhouse and our community. William is a new friend I met on Clubhouse, who resets a room like nobody's business! He knows how to lift people up, knowing as we lift each other up, we all rise up together.

I instantly connected with him when he helped me moderate a friend's room one evening. When I read the line about how "a rising tide lifts all boats" on his profile, I knew he was one of us, and we were instant friends!

> *Club Tip: What to think about while you wait for your invite to Clubhouse...*

Before you join Clubhouse, think carefully about your username because once you choose it, you can only change it once!

Most people use their legal names. They've recently allowed brands to use their Brand / Alias as their name.

You'll notice how both Alicia and Angie's usernames are their full names: @AliciaLyttle and @AngieNorris, while Deb's is what she's known for @CoachDeb instead of her first and last name. Her clients and followers have known her as @CoachDeb since she wrote the 1st book on Twitter back in 2008, and she is @CoachDeb everywhere, so that's what she goes by on Clubhouse.

The advice we give is to try and use the same username you use on all your other social media platforms, so you'll be easily found by your friends, followers and clients. The username is searchable, and ranks in google search now.

You also want to think about what you will be known for on the app. People will be attracted to or turned off by the things you say, so consider how you will show up and what impression you'd like to leave when you exit a chat.

How To Send A Clubhouse Invite
Now that you're in the great inner circle, you may want to invite a friend.

- To invite someone to Clubhouse, they must first be in your phone contacts.
- Grant Clubhouse access to your contacts. Once you've done so, you will see a list of your available contacts to whom you can send an invitation.

- When you send the invite, the recipient will see a text message letting them know you have invited them and the phone number that they should use when they accept the offer.

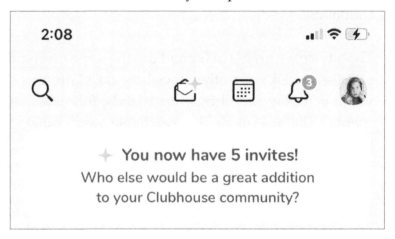

- UPDATE: As I edit this first edition of the Clubhouse Guidebook, the founders just announced during today's Townhall meeting that you can now simply invite someone using their phone number, without having to connect the app to your contacts. Yay! Progress!

Clubhouse App is getting better each and every week as each beta tester suggests features they'd love to see in the app, including better features to help people with visual impairments and for my friends who are deaf or hard of hearing.

Rachelle Dooley @DeafIninitelyMe we hear you and we're listening. Your voice matters. Keep sharing!!

CHAPTER 7:
THE SECRETS TO SETTING UP A STAND OUT PROFILE

When we started using the app, it was mostly trial and error in figuring the platform's ins and outs. Of course, we wish someone had given us these tips and tricks to create an excellent Clubhouse profile and save us time. Why?

Your Clubhouse profile is essential to building your brand and establishing authority in your niche. So let's talk about each section.

Profile photo:
You can use a photo from your camera roll or take a new photo. Whatever you decide, ensure that the picture:

- Shows your face clearly and is well framed. It doesn't hurt to smile.
- Looks great in various sizes as this will be the only one shown throughout the app.
- Has a bright background that contrasts with you. Clubhouse's background colors are white/off-white and light-beige, so it shouldn't be too hard for your photo to pop. Unlike your username, you are allowed to change your profile image as often as you like.

We change our profile photos and bios often, but here's what they looked like at the time of writing this book.

You'll have fun checking out our profiles now in the  app. We keep learning, testing the audience, and revising.

PLUS – we learn a lot from our friends who share their favorite tips in our Club and on our blog.

NOTE: These images are best seen on the Kindle version (and by checking them out directly in the Clubhouse app.

Have I mentioned how much I love our Clubhouse Community?

You can also tailor the background color to your brand style guide.

Club Tip:

To make your profile picture pop, use https://www.remove.bg to remove a busy background, then upload to a free design tool like www.canva.com and make the background a bright color like the yellow Alicia chose for her profile picture.

@CoachDeb (Deborah Cole)
@coachdeb

2434 followers **1589** following

🦃 Author of the 1st Book 🦃 on Twitter 2008
📖 Author of the 1st Book on social media influence 2006

🔮 Coaching Realtors and small business owners since 2001 to get more clients online ... using VIDEO Marketing

🎬 7-Figure Video Marketing Coach
🎬 Video Producer for Real Estate Agents and Small Business Owners

🎬✅😊 Producing a Show for Larry King = highlight of my video production career

🎬✅ 6.8 M $ Launch 🚀 using LIVE Video for GrooveFunnels

🎬✅ Producer of Record breaking 14-Day / 24/7 LIVE Stream

🎬 Helping you to grow your business online with the best tools, tips and secrets to make more sales and get more clients - using video marketing and social media strategies that work.

———

Helping Busy Business Owners produce 7-Figure Video Funnels and getting them to do more LIVE Videos with a simple and easy to follow system without all the tech headaches.

1stMinuteMedia.com

NYC / NJ 🔄 Hawaii 🔄 San Diego

Author of 📖 1st Book on Twitter, predicted how the tool would one day be used by Hollywood, Celebrity Athletes, Business Owners and yes even Presidents to share unfiltered conversations and reach the masses. ((Hey ‼️ Don't kill the messenger. 🔮))

FAQ: "What kind of Coach Are You CoachDeb?"

Business Coach with focus on video + social media marketing.

Peak Performance Coach = Think of me as Your Maggie Siffs helping you reach your maximum potential regardless of the obstacles you face. (minus the leather pants. Cuz ya know... pants are over rated in 2020 🔮 😊 😂 ♥️ 😊

HOBBIES:

🏋️🏋️🏋️ Did someone say Peloton 🚴 ?

Tennis 🎾 Sunset 🌅 Boat ⛵ ?

"It's all about Lifestyle 🏖️ ... AND The Hustle" ✅

🏊 Optimist 🦃 Author 📺 Show Host looking to interview guests who are doing something that's #ShareWorthy or offer a unique perspective. (ShareThisChannel.com)

Champion of the Small Business Owner. Speaker for large companies. (CoachDeb.TV)

Helping people grow their business online and thrive 👍 ♥️ more than ever in 2020.

NEED A WEBSITE?
Need a membership site?
Need a shopping store?

Get your Free Website Builder now at ⚡ GrooveSell.VIP 👍 😊 👍

———

Real estate investing for passive revenue since 1994

YES to all of the above! 😊 ♥️ 😂

Connect with me @CoachDeb everywhere social (Twitter + IG + YouTube —- and Deborah Cole on FB + LinkedIn

New to Clubhouse ?
⚡ Join us on Facebook & we'll get you started fast in the group

✅ 👍 www.ClubhouseConversions.com 👍 ✅
🐦 CoachDeb 📷 coachdeb

🎖️ Joined Aug 30, 2020
   Nominated by **Jeremiah Owyang**

Member of

Angie Norris
@angienorris

1310 followers   **737** following

CEO | Speaker | Coach | Mom
Certified Groove Ambassador
Advanced Online Marketer
Software & Funnel Evangelist

Join my club:
GROOVE CLUB
Master Funnels, Software
& Affiliate Marketing

I have a passion for helping people!!!
Let's connect: AngieNorris.com

20 Year Corporate Director Level
Marketing Veteran

1st Certified Groove Ambassador
GetGrooveFunnelsFree.com

Co-Author of Clubhouse Guidebook with Deborah
Cole & Alicia Lyttle

Top Female Affiliate For Groove

Founder, Funnel Training Channel, TVpreneurs
Entertainment Network & GrooveStars Ascend

Sold over a half a million in expected gross sales
within 90 days

Co-Author of *The Entrepreneur's Playbook,
Overcoming Adversity Through Entrepreneurship, Million
Dollar Story II, and Clubhouse Guidebook*

Visit GrooveRox.com to access the Facebook post
that made me over $50k in expected commission
within 60 days organically.

#Groove GrooveAffiliate #GrooveSell #GrooveVideo
#GrooveMember #GrooveMail

Wine Lover.   Software Junkie.
Empire Builder.

angienorris11   angienorris11

Joined Dec 19, 2020
Nominated by @CoachDeb

Alicia Lyttle
@alicialyttle

2624 followers   **710** following

Speaker / Coach / Digital Marketer / I help people
to build their online EMPIRE! 8 Figures Online
www.AliciaLyttle.net - Free Discovery call. Let's chat

Join our Free Webinar "Online Business Models You
Can Start Today " Visit
www.TheLearningTube.com or text 'newbie' to
888-441-3634

7 Figure digital agency owner
making money w/ Airbnb (SuperHost)
making money selling courses online
7 figure Affiliate Marketer

Won a Mustang Mach -E in the Groove Funnels
affiliate contests.

In Atlanta

alicialyttle   alicialyttle

Joined Oct 28, 2020

Your bio

The first three lines of your Clubhouse profile are the most important as they are the first ones other members will see before expanding your profile to read more. So you want to capture people's attention immediately with these three lines.

Here are a few of the best practices we suggest to our clients for writing your bio.

- Keep it concise
- Use power words to highlight your skills and value that you'll bring to the platform
- Include a strong Call-To-Action (CTA) like Connect with me at (Instagram handle)
- You may include the topics you are interested in, using appropriate keywords to make it easier for users to find you via Member Search.
- Use emojis to separate sections and add pizzazz to your profile.
- If you want to be known and invited to other clubs for a particular area of interest (eg. podcaster, coach, entrepreneur, investor, Realtor, etc), put the term in your profile a few times. When people search for the particular keyword, your profile will pop up. This helps you to gain authority in that niche.

Take a look at this awesome profile that is killing it

with the right use of emojis, hashtags, and unique sections.

Here's what we absolutely love about Mr. Banks' profile:

- Mr. Banks' services are based on credit repair, and he uses several calls-to-action (CTAs) on his profile to ensure it's easy for followers to connect with him.

- His first CTA is to text the 'fire' emoji or #creditit to get a copy of his book.

- He follows this with more CTAs for users to either text emojis or

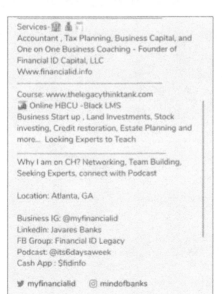

hashtags to get even more information and cool stuff!

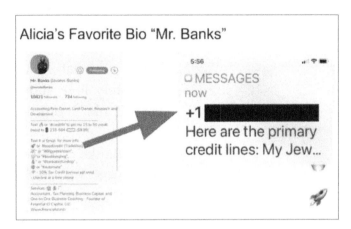

When we texted the rocket ship emoji, we got a text with the message on the right. Cool, right?!

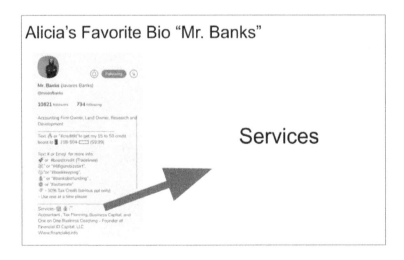

Below his CTAs, he has another section where he lists all the services that he offers as well as his course, location, and the reasons he is on Clubhouse.

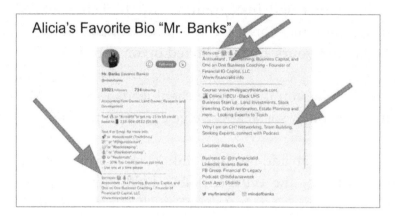

He completes this fantastic Bio by dropping his Cash App, just in case you need it LOL.

We have no doubt that you can make your Bio as cool as Mr. Banks'.

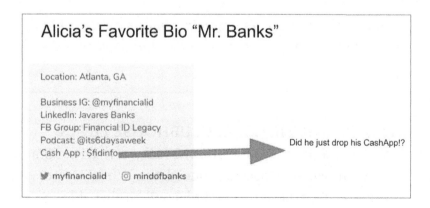

Clickable Links:
There is no inbox and no way for other members to send you a DM on Clubhouse directly.

Both Twitter and Instagram are the backchannels of text communication for Clubhouse rooms right now. Make sure yours are both linked up on your bio.

This is how you'll get more client leads in your DM's then any other social app we've ever seen to date.

While you can add multiple links such as your website to your bio, the only clickable links right now on Clubhouse are your Instagram and Twitter accounts.

Club Tip:
The Clubhouse editor allows you to use emojis that stand out - so use them!

Oh and did we mention? Emojis are searchable!

Smart Club members are using emojis on their bios as SEO friendly ways to stand out and get found in search.

OUR PREDICTION FOR CLUBHOUSE LINKS:
We recommend you include the full www URL name for your website because one day... Voila! All of a sudden, all of these profile links will be clickable.

> *Club Tip:*
> *Users won't be able to copy and paste links, so make them short and memorable with a URL shortener or register a domain name that is short and relevant. You can also opt to use one link that takes users to a landing page with all your other links.*

✓ Ensure that both your Twitter and Instagram accounts are connected to Clubhouse if you want others to contact you easily and continue with conversations you started on the app.

✓ Ensure you make it known that your DMs are open if you wish for members to message you. It also helps to make all your links, including the non-clickable ones, stand out with emojis.

CHAPTER 8:
HOW CLUBHOUSE WORKS
(The Walkthrough Guide)

When you first log into Clubhouse, you will be in what is known as the hallway. It shows all the rooms as well as a top menu bar, calendar of events, and a bottom menu bar for creating your own room. Think of this area like the news feed on Facebook.

We will be going through all the icons you see on this screen.

Let's start with your profile, which is the first thing we want you to set up when you get on to Clubhouse.

Your Profile
Click on your profile picture at the top right:

Make sure your picture is clear. Some people use their brand logo as their profile image, but we recommend using a photo of your face.

People tend to connect easier with faces. Also, make sure the background is free of distractions, so you stand out. (See how to do this in Chapter 7 - The Secrets To Setting Up A Killer Profile That Stands Out On Clubhouse.)

Here are examples of our profile images:

Under your profile image, you will see your name.

If you want to change it, click on your name. This screen will pop up next:

Alicia Lyttle
@alicialyttle

2624 followers   **710** following

Change your username?

@alicialyttle

Update

Bear in mind that you can only change your name and username **once**! So be careful when selecting it!

Next, we get into your bio. The first three lines of your bio are the most important as this is what users see before they expand it to read thoroughly.

Remember to use emojis to help your bio stand out on Clubhouse and get found in search.

Here's an example using Alicia's profile:

You can also add Call-To-Actions (CTAs) to your bio to let users know the actions you want them to take.

In this example, Alicia has asked people to join her free webinar that she hosts every Thursday, or they can text the number, which sends them to a website to sign up for the webinar.

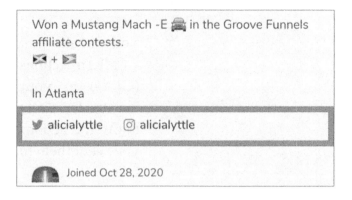

The next step is connecting your Twitter, and Instagram handles. These are the only two clickable links on Clubhouse.

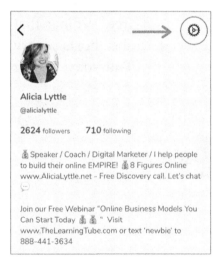

Unfortunately, DMs are not available, so you must ensure that you link these social media accounts so people can connect with you off the platform.

What if you connect the wrong Twitter or Instagram account?

No worries. Click on the gear at the top right corner:

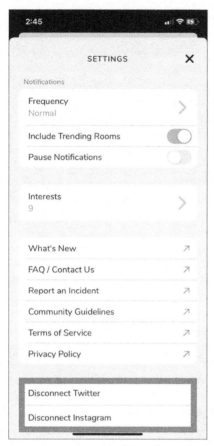

This will take you to "Settings". Now, scroll down to the bottom.

You'll see the options "Disconnect Twitter" and "Disconnect Instagram". Choose the one you wish to change and connect the right account.

At the top of your "Settings" screen, you will "Frequency. This controls the timing of your notifications.

You can also pause notifications coming in by toggling the "Pause Notifications" button.

The recommended frequency is "normal" but if you wish to change it, click the arrow to the right and it will give you options to speed up or slow

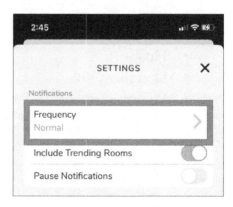

down the timing of your notifications.

Interests

The Interests button takes you to an array of topics that you may find interesting.

Interests are categorized in the following topics:

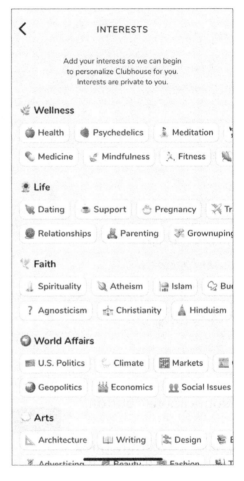

- Wellness
- Life
- Faith
- World Affairs
- Arts
- Sports
- Places
- Tech
- Identity
- Knowledge
- Hustle
- Hanging Out
- Entertainment

Browse the categories and choose topics that you want to know more about.

Fill in your information and click "Done".

Followers and Following

From your bio page, scroll down until you get to Followers. You will see all the people who follow you.

If you want to follow any of these people, click the "Follow" tab to the right of their names.

To know more about any person you want to follow or who

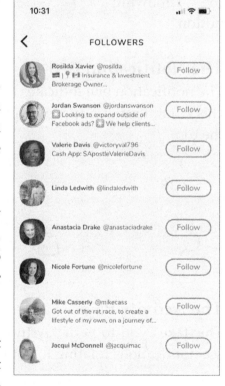

follows you, click on their name to go to their profile:

Now, let's take a look at those you are following. At the top of this screen, you will see the clubs that you are a part of, followed by the people you are following.

If there is someone you wish to stop following, simply click on the "Following" button.

The Notification Bell

The notification bell indicates that you have activity to check out. From your profile page, click on the bell at the top.

The Activity Page

This takes you to your "Activity" page, where you'll see notifications relating to your account.

The Calendar - scheduling rooms

The next icon on your profile page is the calendar.

The calendar is used to schedule events (rooms) and clubs.

To schedule an event, click the calendar icon. This will take you to a tab titled "What would you like to see?". Click the option "My Events".

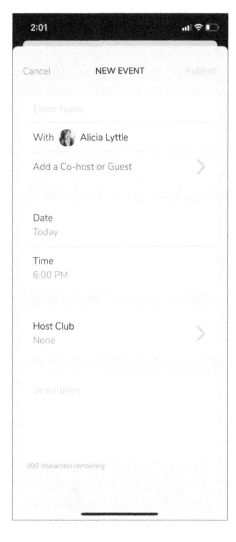

Next, click on the calendar icon at the top right and you will be taken to a page to create your event.

From here, insert your Event Name and add your co-hosts. Include the date and time of your event. You get 200 characters to write a description. Ensure that you write a compelling narrative of what your event/room will be about.

And Use Emojis!

> *Club Tip: Add an emoji at the beginning of your event title and another at about 3-4 words in. Why? Users will be notified by email of your event. The emojis will help your email to stand out and get noticed faster than a plain text email.*

Before adding co-hosts, let them know you want them to co-host a room with you. Give them the time, date and subject you will be discussing so that they can prepare.

When you are finished creating your event, click "Publish".

How To Find And Start An Event

When it's time for your event to start, click on the calendar from your profile page.

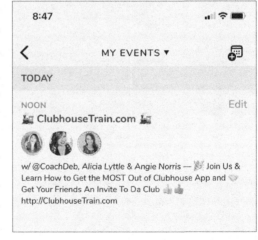

Next, click "My Events" and then click on your scheduled event.

You will see a green button that says "Start Room". Click the button to start the event.

> *Club Tip: Make sure that you are the one who starts the event as the algorithm will recognize you as a host. The more rooms you host, the greater your chances of being allowed to start a Club, getting more invites, and other privileges super users will get over inactive ones. .*

Upcoming Event

From your profile page, click the calendar icon to see "Upcoming For You".

You will see a list of rooms and clubs that will go live at specific times. If you click on one of these rooms, you'll get the options to "Share", "Tweet", "Copy Link" and "Add to Calendar.

- "Share" - this creates a link that you can forward or copy and send via email or message.
- "Tweet" - creates a tweet with your event title, hosts, and link to the event.
- "Copy link" - this will copy the event's URL to your clipboard so you can paste it wherever you wish.

You can remind invitees to click the bell at the top of your profile page to receive notifications each time you speak.

Whenever you create a room, it's important that you market it across social media to get as many people as possible interested to attend your room. Use all the icons to promote your event.

Club Tip: The best way to fill a room fast is to add moderators and influencers who have a large following.

When they are brought to the stage and start talking, their followers will be notified and invited to join the room.

The Envelope

When you click on the envelope on your profile page, you can see how many invites you have. It will look like this:

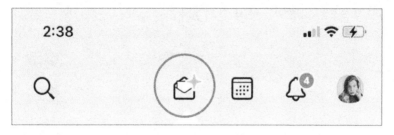

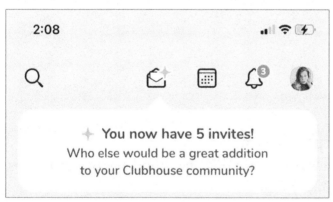

If you want to find a contact in your phone to invite, type their name in the search bar:

Be careful choosing contacts during this process as there is currently no way to get back an invite you send!

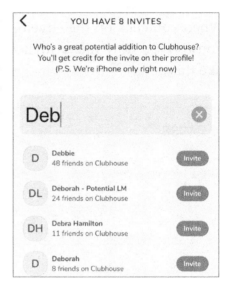

The Explore Icon

Click on the Explore button to find people and clubs you wish to follow.

From here, you can also find topics that others are talking about. Below "Find Conversations About...", click on a category that interests you.

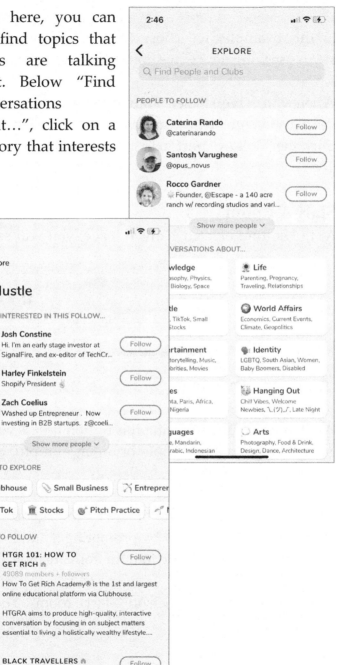

In this example, we chose "Hustle" because we're always seeking new ways for our fans to make money!

When you have chosen your category, you will see people and clubs with conversations around the topic. Click the "Follow" button to get notified when they go live.

Start A Room

At the bottom of your hallway page, you will see the

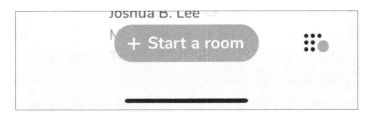

"Start A Room" button.

We don't recommend using this button unless you are going to start a closed room or an impromptu, casual chat with a few friends.

Scheduling a room is the best way to organize your room and get people in it by promoting it and inviting your influential friends to join the conversation.

To start a closed room, click on "Start a room". You will be taken to this tab:

Open - this means anyone can join and is the default setting for every room in Clubhouse.

Social - only those you follow you will be able to join and is easily the option when you want to just have a chat with people you trust. If you want to convert it to an Open room, invite other people as moderators, and their followers will join.

HINT:

The Founders of Clubhouse have been placing special emphasis to these types of "Social Rooms" that are designed to connect one another to their friends for genuine connections. Paul Davison practically gets giddy when he talks about holding these types of rooms, because he knows these are the types of rooms that'll bond you with genuine connections, and therefore, you'll spend more time on the app.

Try these out. You may find they're the most alluring each night, at the end of a long day working, allowing you to joke around with real friends who support you.

PLUS:

These Social Rooms are shown at the top of your friend's hallway, sooooo... you may find you'll connect with people in this way, because your other rooms might get lost in the shuffle with all the rooms and clubs being hosted now that ten million have joined Clubhouse.

Closed - only the people you select will know about the room. This is a perfect choice if you want a more private conversation or want to talk with a smaller group but don't yet have a Club for it (we'll discuss Clubs soon). Once started, you can always Ping in more people or open it up to a Social or Open room, so it's a great conversation starter!

Ensure that you select "Closed" and then click on "Choose People" to select your private members.

Type the name of the person you want to add in the search tab. Note that only you and the invited person will be in the room.

When you're finished talking, close the room by selecting "End room". Otherwise, your room will be left open for anyone to hop on and take over.

Finding Available People

You can find people available to talk by clicking on this icon at the bottom right of your hallway page.

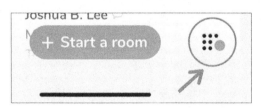

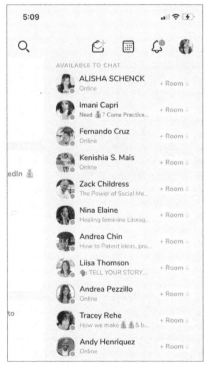

You'll see a list of people currently online. You can hit up any of these people to have a private conversation.

CHAPTER 9:
GET ON STAGE NOW!

Clubhouse rooms listed in your hallway are open rooms where any member is free to join and participate or listen in.

There are two sections within rooms - the stage at the top where the speakers and moderators are; and the audience, which is where most members are when they join a room.

Rooms are managed by moderators who give audience members opportunities to speak.

There are two ways to get on stage: being invited up by one of the moderators on stage, or raising your hand and getting selected to join the panel on stage to either ask your question, or contribute something of value to the conversation.

The Stage

When you tap on a room to enter, you will immediately see the 'Stage' at the top.

This area shows a picture of everyone who is currently on the 'Stage', identified by their first names.

You'll notice the new members who joined clubhouse within the past seven days or less, by the party popper emoji listed in the lower left of their profile picture.

You will also be able to see which members are muted.

All audience members below the stage don't have access to a mic and are muted.

But when you're called up to stage, you enter the stage with a "hot mic" which means any background noise or anything you're saying will be heard by everyone in the room.

So... mute your mic immediately! (or risk certain embarrassment, especially if you're like most people, and hopping on clubhouse while in "your private office" in your home. (aka the bathroom)

How To Mute Your Mic

Simply hit the mic in the lower right hand corner of your app to mute your mic. You'll see a line slash over your mic to indicate you are now on mute.

Mute your mic the moment you get pulled on stage – otherwise a moderator will mute you and potentially drop you back into the audience.

Moderators

Pictures that have the "green bean" icon indicate who the moderators are in the room.

It is always best to have at least one moderator in your room, in case you accidently leave the room, or the app glitches, leaving your room with no moderator to control the rooms or ping you back in.

Moderators are the ones who can pull people up on stage and drop them back into the audience after they're finished asking their question.

Give Moderator access carefully, as you're giving them full control of your room – including the ability to boot you from your own room, or end the room. But a pro moderator will make your room grow and flow.

When someone is speaking on stage, you will see an outline around their picture.

The Audience

Below "The Stage" you'll see two sections.

Immediately under the stage are the members of the audience who are listed to indicate the members "Followed by the speakers."

The next section below that list all the people who don't follow the speakers or aren't being followed by the speakers in the audience section indicated as, "Others in the room".

The audience in open rooms include all room members who are "just visiting" but not necessarily following the speakers or members of the club hosting the room.

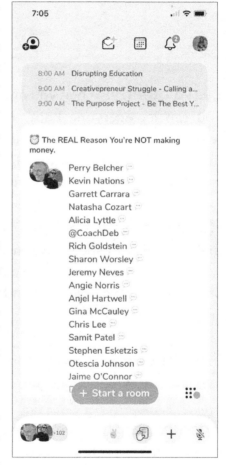

Hallway Lists

You'll see the people you follow in rooms in your hallway as well as others in the room speaking, indicated by the chat icon right after their name.

This feature allows you to see friends who are in rooms that you may want to join and see what the room is discussing.

How To Interact In a Room

You will see the action bar buttons at the bottom of your screen to interact with members in a room. If you are in the audience, you will see these buttons:

Leave quietly: When you are ready to leave a room, you can let everyone know by announcing it (only relevant if you are a key speaker); otherwise, click on the "Leave quietly" button. This allows you to leave the room without notifying anyone that you've left.

Hand Raise: Click on this to let the moderator know that you wish to speak. When you are identified, you will be brought to the 'Stage'. When you're done, tap on your profile picture and click on 'Move to audience'.

Ping Button: Use this to "ping someone" aka invite a friend who follows you into the room.

Microphone: Click on this to mute and unmute your microphone. The term used for an open mic or one that's not muted is called a 'hot mic'. Remember to mute your microphone whenever you're not speaking.

Hot Tip To Get On Stage:

If you really want to get on stage when speakers open it up for questions, here's a great way to get the attention of the moderators selecting who'll be the best person to pull up first:

* Put your question for the speakers at the top of your profile.

* Even better, put the name of the speaker you want to ask your question, then list your question in a concise one to two lines.

* And if you really want to be the first person in the queue, do a little research on the speakers / moderators and put something flattering about them right after the question you list at the top of your profile.

* Speakers want to give attention to their fans and clients first, because they're the ones supporting the creators sharing their knowledge freely during these open rooms.

* Oh, and if you're not following the speaker or moderator, you not only run the risk of not getting pulled up, you run the risk of insulting the speaker you are trying to seek help from.

Hot Tip From Podcast Magazine Founder, Steve Olsher Reveals:

"One of the things that we love to do to reinforce the brand of the club and encourage people to 'show love for the club' while they are in one of our rooms is to change over their profile picture to the ClubPod image.

We incentivize them to do so by saying that we will first open the stage for questions for people who change their image to ClubPod's. Of course it isn't mandatory but a lot of people do it to skip the line. It looks incredible when you see a stage full of your club logo."

Steve Olsher

Here is what a room looks like when everyone on stage "shows love for the club" when Pat Flynn, Founder of Smart Passive Income Podcast was the guest speaker.

CLUBPOD 🏠   • • •

Pat Flynn Of SPI! LIVE Q&A {Recording 🔴}

✳ Steve   ✳ Pat   Juliet

Julie   Justin   Dr.

Teri   Shawn   Vanika

Coaches Corner:

A book written by @CoachDeb wouldn't be complete without an Action Sheet in it with things you can do to get on stages in Clubhouse, now would it?

Take a moment for yourself to list the clubs and rooms you want to take a more active role in and contribute to or ask your favorite celebrity or influencer.

My Action Sheet For Getting On More Stages:

Clubs I want to get on stage:

Rooms I can create and run my own stage:

Influencers I want to invite to join me on stage:

CHAPTER 10:
START YOUR CLUB TODAY

In addition to rooms you can start and run, and get on stages of your own, Clubhouse also has Clubs, which are communities created around shared interests.

While rooms are open to everyone, Club membership is determined by admins and one can qualify for a Club only after they have run at least three rooms themselves and have mastered moderating rooms.

You can identify a Club by the green house icon next to a room title. Clubs can be private or public. Club members usually have "Member of" badges on their profiles.

Clubs you have started are listed first in the list of Clubs you are a member of. You'll see all the Clubs you're a member of or run at the bottom of your profile.

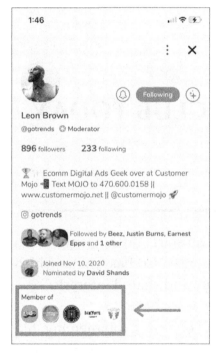

How To Find And Join A Club

Clubhouse doesn't currently have a Clubs directory, but the creators hope to have one soon.

Meanwhile, the best way to find a Club is via conversations, looking for them on the events calendar or in your feed, and following members who have club badges on their profiles. You can't request to join a Club now, but many of them allow you to follow them so that you will be notified each time they have a public event.

How To Start A Club

Members can only create Clubs if they have been active on the app for one month and scheduled at least three events or rooms in a row with the same topic. This shows consistency to the Clubhouse founders, showing them you're serious about running a club.

EXCITING UPDATE!

We are updating this book for you right now with the following exciting updates about starting clubs, now that you can do it directly in the app itself!

When this book was first published on 1/21/21 the only way to get a club was to submit an application, and this chapter was dedicated to our members to walk them through the strategy to get your club approved.

Well now it's easier than ever because you simply need to scroll down to the bottom of your profile where you see all your clubs. Flick all the clubs to the left until you get to the last club you're a member of. That's where you'll see a little + sign. Simply hit that plus + sign and create your club!

Since we imagine this feature will change and adapt, we created a video walking you through this process and shared it on the blog.

Just enter "Start A Club" in the search for ClubhouseConversations.com and you'll see the article with the video walking you through the step by step process, with a few strategic tips to think about when naming your club and whether or not to make it public or private.

The one thing to note if you don't see that + sign at the end of your clubs, because it may be because you're new to the app and have never started and run a room yet, or it simply means you need to update your phone or the app itself to make sure you've got the latest versions and are up to date to see that new feature added to Clubhouse.

Coaches Corner:

New Club Planning

Here are a few items you'll want to have a strategy for and be prepared with a description of your club in a separate note taking service like Evernote or your Notes on your phone to easily copy/paste when starting your new club.

Jot down your ideas here in this book to brainstorm a few ideas and think strategically when considering each item.

- Club name
  <50 characters. This must include text (e.g. cannot be just numbers; no emojis or other special characters.)

- Club category / Topics
  Note you can only select 3 topics. So choose the top three topics you'll focus all your rooms around.

- Description of club
  This will be displayed on the club page in the app. Add emojis to separate sections creatively.

- Will you allow followers?

- Will you let members start rooms?

- Will you make your member list private?

Start A Club Now – It's So Easy Now!

If you're a Speaker, Author or Podcaster, you need to start your own Club. It's a no brainer. And if you're a business owner interested in connecting with people and meeting new clients you can help, I'd highly encourage you to think about starting a cool club to bring people together, and share your expertise.

(Oh, and yes! We are beyond excited about how much easier this is for all our clients creating their own club.)

Here are the screen shots to show you the process of starting a new Club. For this example, I'm creating a brand new club that will more than likely, become the Daily Show I run. But for now, it's simply your example as I updated this chapter at 9:45pm and needed to show you screenshots. LOL

Watch how fast the process is by the time captured from these screen shots.

- ✓ Name Your Show
- ✓ Enter Your Description (copy/paste from notes)
- ✓ Don't Allow Followers YET (Big Tip I'll explain why in a minute)
- ✓ Invite Your Business Besties (aka Partners)
- ✓ Add 3 Club Topics
- ✓ Upload A Logo (Or Cool Image)
- ✓ BOOM! Done! Now Schedule Your First Event

FIRST: Name your Club! Think "Show" and you'll win on Clubhouse. Think in threes! Try to name your Club in three words or less. Four words max if needed.

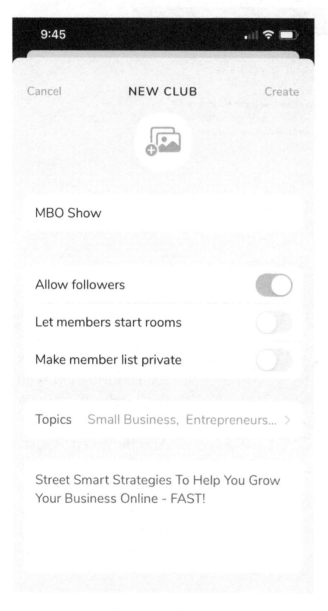

NEXT: Invite your top ten besties to your club by typing their name in the search box and click that blue INVITE Button.

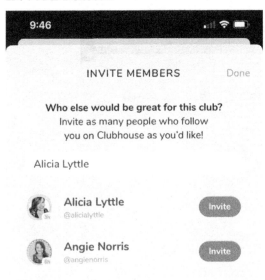

Voila!

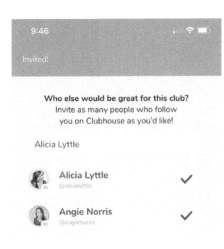

You'll immediately see confirmation with the check mark they've been invited. And the green "Toast" Notifcation will pop up on your screen giving you confirmation your invites went through.

Easy, right?

LAST: Choose your top three topics that your Club (Show) will focus on each time you meet. DONE!

Notice the time stamps in my screenshot? Fast, eh?

CONGRATULATIONS! If you followed these three to four steps with me, you've now got your own Club! And now all you need to do – is schedule your first event (considered "a room") in Clubhouse.

The next part of your club setup is the strategic part.

Client conversations around Clubs have been focused around the following questions to consider and decide upon when launching your own Club.

Take a moment to strategize the following:

➢ Whether or not to keep your club private or open it to the public where anyone can join?

➢ Should you allow your members to run rooms in your club?

➢ Will you hire a pro moderator to run your Club rooms with you?

➢ Or will you select moderators from your Club to be moderators for each event scheduled?

Once you've created your Club in the app, your next steps are "making it a lil fancy" and inviting members.

If you are opening your Club up to the public, you'll want to do a few things to attract your tribe.

First, upload your logo. If you don't have a logo for it, you can simply upload your profile pic or have a little fun in Canva to upload an image that best represents your Club topics.

See how much prettier your club is with your logo in at that top?

Next, you'll want to add a more in depth description for your club, and describe the perfect member for your club so you attract the right people who'll be an asset to your club followers.

In just a minute, I'll show you how I did this for my other club I started earlier this month. But for now, you're all set with your first club.

See how easy the process is?

For this particular club, I decided I need to do a DAILY SHOW!

Wait... What?!

Yup, I figured if I could show up for a daily television show Monday through Friday, (and that show required pants and lipstick!) then I should be able to dedicate an hour a day for my clients, followers, fans and friends on an audio only app. Right?

GULP. Ok, now I'm sweating a bit as I realize I'm making this very public commitment.

Perhaps I'd feel guilty if I didn't do it, like I'm keeping all this wisdom to myself with access to all the amazing, smart, influential friends I've got who each have such incredible tips on growing your influence on social media they are happy to share with you.

But I will need your help to make this daily show continue more than the next 30 days I'm committed to doing.

So… are you up for helping and joining in?

If you'd make an Awesome Guest, I'd love to hear from you and get you on my Daily Show. You can just eMail my producer to set something up: ClubhouseConversations@gmail.com

And if you simply want to join me every day in the MBO Show Club, I can't wait to meet you and hear how this book has helped you succeed on Clubhouse. When you would invite a few friends to join you each day, and I notice a genuine interest for me to continue sharing business tips each day, I'll keep the room going as long as you'd like.

Afterall, the amazing Angie Norris has been holding her daily room for 100+ days now. She started it over the holiday break as 2020 year was finally coming to an end, and she hasn't stopped.

Hot Tip From Angie For Club Management:

Angie is smart with the moderation and management of her daily room, because she found five other moderators to take the lead each day to help run her room: Purpose Project. Follow her lead if you don't want to get overwhelmed running shows in your Club.

Ok, now that you've got your club started, it's time to create your Club's Mission. Clubhouse calls this a description, and you can revise it as often as you'd like.

I highly recommend you type up your description in an app like Evernote. This gives you a nice saved copy that you can revise and refine as you grow your club. I also recommend having a few different versions to test and see what attracts the best member when you're running your club events.

The next page shows you an example of a Club description from what I created for the new Club I created specifically to bring influential Podcasters together to interview them along with Influencers and Celebrities for my new podcast.

NOTE to keep in mind when creating your description: My new podcast is called "Clubhouse Conversations" to indicate the conversations record in Clubhouse to share on the podcast for people who aren't in Clubhouse so they won't miss out on the wealth of knowledge shared by these leaders I'm interviewing.

BUT... Clubhouse will not allow you to use the word "Clubhouse" in a Club name. So, I simply called the Club: "Podcast Conversations" to indicate this show is for the new podcast and will be inviting my guests to join and connect with other podcasters on Clubhouse.

Creating the right description for your club

Remember: Emojis are not just fun to break up the text; they're also searchable and will help you with discoverability on the app.

PODCAST CONVERSATIONS

➡️ Where Podcasters, Celebrities and YouTubers gather to share their best tips, hacks and secrets of podcasting, video production and online marketing.

🔘 Interviews with Influencers
🔘 Interviews with Celebrities
🔘 Interviews with Experts

✅ Are you looking to book yourself to be interviewed on podcasts?

✅ Are you a host of a podcast looking for awesome speakers to interview on your podcast?

🎇 This is the Club where you connect and collaborate.

✳️🔘 Host your Podcast Conversations in this Club & share the time of your Show on the Clubhouse Conversations Blog & Facebook Group: Clubhouse Conversions.

NOTE: Interviews from this series may be included in the next book on Clubhouse. (only the best ones)

Invite Members To Your Club:

HOT TIP as you invite members to your club... Invite your top ten members in first. BEFORE you open up your Club to the general public. Choose the friends and business partners and clients who support you the most. These top ten members that'll be listed right underneath you should be folks who best represent what your club is all about, and willing to help you grow the club together.

Your top ten members will be the ones all future members will see as they find your club and join it. These top ten members will be helping you manage the club and grow the club. They will also receive a ton of followers in return, because people tend to follow the top ten people in your club.

This is a tip we learned the hard way when we opened our first club to the public. Fortunately, we were lucky that we've got awesome friends who joined our club first, and are now forever listed in the top ten!

Members vs Followers: The Difference

The difference is that Members of your club can also open up rooms under your club brand and see one another to follow each other. Whereas Followers only see your club and get alerted when you or any of your members run a room under your club and can join the room.

Hot Club Tip For Your Profile:

Remember how we've been talking about how the first three lines in your profile are the most important?

Well, now we've noticed the app is only showing the first two lines of your profile narrative!

Did you notice that in the last image we shared of the Members of Podcast Conversations?

That's how you'll show up in Club rooms. So choose your first two lines carefully to reflect your brand and who you are looking to attract and connect with in Clubhouse.

I recommend my clients to mix it up a bit. Try different things in the first two lines and see what works best.

You may even want to ask a connection building question in this first line to connect with people you really want to meet.

For example:
Are You a Podcaster?
I'd love to meet you!

CHAPTER 11:
HOW TO FIND YOUR CLUB
ON THE APP

- When you have completed your Club setup, go to your Clubhouse profile. You'll see the terms "Member of" and the club "badge".

- Click on the badge and it will take you to the Club page. You should see your name listed as a member. Congratulations! Remember that as the Club creator, you are by default a founder or admin.

Adding Someone As A Co-Founder (or Admin) To Your Club

- You can add Club members as co-founders. To do this, go to the Club profile and select the member you wish to make co-founder.

- You will see the option to "make an admin".

- You may also remove someone as a founder from this page.

As A Club Founder, You Should Know

Types of Clubs - A Club can comprise founders, members, and followers.

- **Founders/Admins** - are responsible for choosing who to invite and add as members as well as start public Club-branded rooms. They can also change the club description, rules, and icon and vet members for entry from members' suggestions.

- **Members** - cannot choose invitees but can nominate people to join. The Club's founder must review and accept or reject them. Members can also start private Club-branded rooms, which will only be seen by Club members and Admins.

- **Followers** - are not able to create rooms and can only see public Club rooms. They will, however, receive notifications when the Club schedules a public room.

How To Invite People To Join Your Club

To add a member, simply click on the icon at the top right of the Club page. You'll see four options:

- Copy secret invite link: share this link with someone whose phone number you don't have.

- Review nominated members: members who are not founders can make suggestions for new members that founders must approve.

- Search Clubhouse: you are privy to inviting anyone on Clubhouse who follows you.

- Search contacts: Invite anyone off Clubhouse who is on your contact list. This will use your allotted club invites.

Clubhouse Invitations

Invitations are allocated automatically based on how much you contribute to the community. Host great conversations with your Club as often as possible and invites will automatically appear in your account!

You'll receive in-app notifications when invites are made available to you.

How To Add A Club Event To The Calendar

To schedule your Club's event on the in-app Calendar, tap the Calendar icon from the home screen. Then tap the + icon in the top right and fill out the details requested.

How To Co-host With Another Club

You can't formally include more than one Club as an event host on the Calendar but many Clubs don't allow this to stop them from collaborating informally. Once an event has started, founders of Clubs can invite their members by tapping the "+" icon at the bottom of the room and selecting the Club.

NEW Feature Just Added!

Now you can share a direct link to both your profile and your club. Just hit the setting tab in your Club and look for the option to copy or share the link. BOOM!

Clubhouse just made it easier for you to share your link on your other social accounts or via text message for your friends to find you easily or join your club quickly through your direct link.

Hot Club Tip by Steve Olsher, Founder of Podcast Magazine on ways to get on stage and get the attention of the Club Creator or Host:

"ONE OF THE THINGS THAT WE LOVE TO DO TO REINFORCE THE BRAND OF THE CLUB AND ENCOURAGE PEOPLE TO 'SHOW LOVE FOR THE CLUB' WHILE THEY ARE IN ONE OF OUR ROOMS IS TO CHANGE OVER THEIR PROFILE PICTURE TO THE CLUBPOD IMAGE.

WE INCENTIVIZE THEM TO DO SO BY SAYING THAT WE WILL FIRST OPEN THE STAGE FOR QUESTIONS FOR PEOPLE WHO CHANGE THEIR IMAGE TO CLUBPOD'S. OF COURSE, IT ISN'T MANDATORY BUT A LOT OF PEOPLE DO IT. IT LOOKS INCREDIBLE WHEN YOU SEE A STAGE FULL OF YOUR CLUB LOGO."

Here's an example of what a room looks like in ClubPod when members "show love for the club" when Pat Flynn, Founder of Smart Passive Income Podcast was on as a guest speaker.

CHAPTER 12:
CONNECT WITH INFLUENCERS

The highlight of Clubhouse since the Summer of 2020 has been the Saturday night dinner parties hosted by well-known philanthropist Felicia Horowitz.

Revolving around buzz-worthy topics, the parties usually pull in no less than 100 members, including the who's who of the 'glitterati. Here, they talk with each other, discussing current events,  sharing stories, just like... an IRL dinner party.

Following

Terry Crews

@terrycrews

10.1k followers   **182** following

In the room, celebrities spotted include Oprah Winfrey, former New York Yankees pitcher CC Sabathia, Dallas Cowboys linebacker Jaylon Smith, former pro football player Marcellus Wiley, Los Angeles Lakers center Javale McGee, MC Hammer, Terry Crews, and LL Cool J.

Of note was one Saturday evening when E40 shared a history-making event of musicians inspiring souls with their talent during the 2020 lockdowns.

He spoke about playing tunes when he was stuck in LA after coming home from Minnesota visiting with his daughter. And then the unforgettable day Michelle

Obama came on to listen to him create music for the world!

Epic, historic events - that happened with people from all over the world on Instagram LIVE and talked about on Clubhouse.

MC HAMMER
@gigahamm

31.6k followers   **997** following

As rival apps rise up to compete with an audio platform of their own, I'm asked if Clubhouse will win or fade in the distance like Blab. And my answer varies, but always focused around the Vibe that Clubhouse has that none of these other competitors have figured out yet.

I believe… Felicia has a lot to do with setting that tone for the app… since the early days, with these informal conversations with celebrities, musicians, and investors that join her virtual dinner party every Saturday evening starting at 5pm PST.

Highly recommend following Felicia's Virtual Dinner
Party Club so you'll see her rooms in your hallway.

FELICIA'S VIRTUAL DINNER PARTY

Following

Every Saturday at 5:00pm: Felicia's Virtual Dinner
Party is a curation of high-quality conversations
covering issues to pique our curiosity.

Dinner guests include visionaries from science,
business, politics, technology, food, sports, culture,
and more!

Come pull up a seat and join the conversation with
diverse leaders from all walks of life.

📺 Television · 🍎 Education · 🏆 The Future

50 Members

 Felicia Horowitz @feliciahorowitz
Virtual Dinner Party Host 🍷 Following

 Tanya Sam @tanya
Angel investor. Real Housewife 🏠
😊. Oncology RN to tech. Biblioph... Following

 Ben Horowitz @bentonio
Andreessen Horowitz
Author of The Hard Thing About H... Following

 Terry Crews @terrycrews
Terry Crews is an action-movie hero,
sitcom star, children's book illustrat... Following

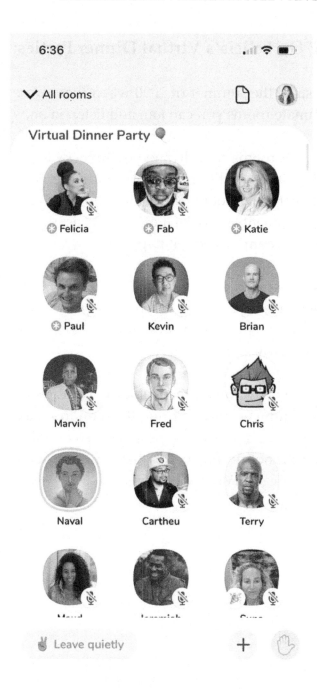

UPDATE On Felicia's Virtual Dinner Parties:

Long past since the summer of 2020 when these were smaller intimate rooms you can join and listen in on.

These days, her rooms are full, and you're lucky to get in the room with 8,000 listening in the audience. So if you want to get in her room, be sure to follow her club and join the moment she kicks it off. Otherwise... you can't get in the room... where it happens.

The app is growing... and will continue to grow. You want to get in early, get on often, and grow your influence and connect with influencers before it's saturated and grows in difficulty.

Club Tip: If you want more people in your room, connect with influencers, and bring them on to speak. This will alert their followers, especially if you remind people to hit the notification bell to "Always" so they'll know when you go LIVE in Clubhouse.

CHAPTER 13:
GROW YOUR BUSINESS ON CLUBHOUSE

If you own a business and you're not focused on building a strong brand presence and growing your business on Clubhouse, your customers are already choosing your competitors.

No lies!

Mr. Banks (Javares Banks)
@mindofbanks

10821 followers   **734** following

Accounting Firm Owner, Land Owner, Research and Development

Text 🔥 or "#creditlit"to get my 15 to 50 credit boost to 📱 218-504-0512 ($9.99)

Text # or Emoji for more info:
💳 or #boostcredit (Tradelines)
🎯 " or "#6figurebizstart",
📚 "or "#bookkeeping",
💰 " or "#banksbizfunding",
⚙️ or "#automate"
💵 - 30% Tax Credit (serious ppl only)
- Use one at a time please

Services- 🏦 💰 📑
Accountant , Tax Planning, Business Capital, and One on One Business Coaching - Founder of Financial ID Capital, LLC
Www.financialid.info

We have seen members increase their brand visibility by more than 100% and quadruple their monthly sales quota in a single day just from one substantial conversation in a chatroom.

The minute you start speaking and adding value to a room, you'll begin to attract an audience that identifies with you and your brand. Before you even stop talking, they will head over to your profile to check you out.

So how do you leverage Clubhouse to grow your business and convert leads?

Complete Your Winning Profile

Remember we said that audience members would run to your profile to know more about you? This means your bio has to be on point!

Ensure you create a killer Bio (follow the tips we gave in Chapter 3 - The secrets to setting up a killer profile that stands out on Clubhouse). Next, transform your bio into a digital business card!

Here's how:

Set up a Linktree (a personalized and easily-customizable page that houses all the links you want to share with your audience.)

Next, copy your unique Linktree URL and paste it in your bio. This link will take your audience to your series of services or product suite.

Build Value, Authority And Expertise

Clubhouse has gained as much traction as it has because of the types of conversations people can have within its rooms.

Conversations are interesting, purposeful, and valuable. The most memorable speakers are always those who willingly share useful information and ideas that add value to their listeners.

You don't have to be proactive with a sales pitch.

Don't try to sell to members while you're speaking.

Simply bring your expertise to a topic and share something that is not easily found on Google.

A useful tip is to have listeners silently make micro-commitments as you speak. Ask them leading questions that set the stage for your product or service.

Let them imagine a better experience with more of your knowledge and expertise. The more commitments you can get them to make, the more they will want to engage with your brand.

SEO your profile

Treat your Clubhouse bio like your website or other social media pages - optimize with power keywords.

Try to get those keywords in the first and second sentences. For example, if you are a digital marketer, you could use branding, social media, and marketing in your bio. When people search for those terms, your bio will pop up.

Network And Collaborate

Clubhouse is an awesome app for networking. You're able to connect with people who crave information and who share similar business interests.

The fact that moguls, icons, business owners, and successful entrepreneurs are so willing to give out free nuggets of information to help you grow your business is a huge plus.

So get to networking! Bear in mind that your vibe attracts your tribe. Follow the people you believe can genuinely bring value to your business.

When you get into a room, don't just listen - participate! Ask questions and bounce ideas.

The great thing is that the experts will answer your questions right then and there. If you get the opportunity to re-room with an expert, go for it!

Remember that there is no record once a room is closed so your chats are private – unless the RECORDING Icon is in the title of the room and it's recorded for a future podcast.

Add Calls To Action (CTAs) To Your Bio

Don't be afraid to let people know how to contact you. So include terms like FOLLOW ME or DM FOR MORE INFO. Links aren't clickable on Clubhouse, so if you are going to put a link, use a URL shortener to make it memorable.

Connect Your Instagram + Twitter

Wow! You wouldn't believe how many times we have seen people lose out on sales opportunities because they haven't connected these social media accounts.

And to think that these are THE ONLY TWO clickable links allowed on Clubhouse (at the moment)! These are your golden tickets to increase visibility and engagement as well as grow your tribe. People want to connect with you, so make it easy!

Start Your Own Room And Give Something Of Value Away For FREE

When you host a room, you get to decide the topic, speakers, and tone of the conversations. This means you can create a room based on what you offer.

To create excitement and buzz, tell guests that you will give away (something of value to them) if the room gets a certain number of people.

Prompt them to invite others so they can benefit from the gift. In this space, you can feel free to promote your products and services as a follow up to the gift you provided.

Host welcome parties for new members

Suppose you host a scheduled event (which we strongly recommend). In that case, you may find that you are continuously getting new members at each event. After a certain number of new people have joined, host a welcome party to introduce them to longstanding members and make them feel like they belong.

Make your party fun!

Consider inviting a different speaker/moderator to each party and do mini-competitions and giveaways.

You can also make the parties themed and ask members to change their profile image based on the theme.

CHAPTER 14:
CLUBHOUSE ETIQUETTE

If you behave well and follow Clubhouse's rules, you are more likely to be a raging success on the platform.

- Respect the members of a room. Be open-minded and ready to learn. Remember that someone's opinion is just that, and everyone is entitled to have and voice them - especially in an audio-only social app!

- Some rooms may have themes or topics, while others don't. Be open to topic changes. Remember, these are live conversations, so expect the usual ebb and flow of a face-to-face discussion with like-minded people.

- If you are not speaking, stay muted not to disturb speakers with background noise or echo.

- If you appreciate a speaker, you can "clap" them by muting and unmuting fast.

- You're likely to hear Clubhouse members say "PTR" quite often. This means "pull to refresh' and is used to refresh a page to show new people entering a room or when you're changing your profile picture.

- When given a chance to speak, make your point clearly and succinctly.

- If you're in a large room and wish to continue the conversation with select individuals, you can "re-room". To do this, tap on the person(s) profile picture and click on "Start a new room together," or you can start a new room and then ping the people you want to join.

CHAPTER 15:
MODERATOR TIPS FOR RUNNING ROOMS AND GROWING THEM

Rooms on Clubhouse are managed by moderators. They are responsible for setting the tone and conversation within a group, among other activities.

There are two ways to become a moderator:

- Create a room
- Get an invitation from another moderator to promote you from an audience member

As a moderator, you can:
- Mute/unmute speakers

- Bring speakers to the stage
- Accept requests from audience members to speak
- Promote speakers to moderators

Each room needs a moderator to chime in every 10-15 minutes to "Reset the room," especially as new people join. Think about this like a radio show where you welcome new listeners and tell them what the discussion topic is.

Room Reset Tips

Perry Belcher, one of the early adopters and founders of Digital Marketing, is an excellent Clubhouse host and speakers on Clubhouse. (Even at 5:30am PST Monday mornings when he runs his Marketing Meeting rooms.)

Perry has now hired a pro moderator to run his rooms and help manage it, so he can focus on sharing his tips on sales and marketing.

The BEST Moderator I've ever seen "reset a room" and met on Clubhouse is William Tong. He helped me run Perry's room one day when the room just kept running and no one wanted it to end.

Here's an example of how William Tong would reset Perry's room every 10-15 minutes:

"Hi, welcome to (Perry's room).

We are talking about (topic).

Everyone can PTR or pull to refresh so you'll see the new speakers to follow and who's in the audience."

He'll then go on to remind everyone to follow those on the stage.

"...and hit the bell to be notified when they speak again in the future. Be sure to check out their profiles and follow them on Twitter & Instagram to stay in touch."

He then instructs them on how to ask questions:

"Please tell us what your question is by starting with, "My question is". Remember, we don't need to know your whole life story. We want to respect everyone's time, so you'll have approximately 28 seconds to ask your question."

Stage Management Tips

When the person's question is answered, tap on their profile picture and click on 'Move to audience' to move them from the stage and make way for someone else to speak.

You can tell the room members that if they hear a killer tip, PING a friend who would LOVE to know because their friends will thank them for bringing them into the BEST room on Clubhouse.

Secret Club Tip To Control Your Stage:

Sometimes, people who are permitted to come to the stage ignore the brevity rule or are just plain rude/disrespectful. As the moderator, you can bump them back into the audience and blame it on audio interference - LOL. I've seen mods do this more than once.

Growth Hacking Tip For Clubhouse Rooms

PING Influencers to join your room and bring them onto the stage to speak when they come in. This notifies their entire follower base! You can double the number of room members in minutes!

Does this really work?

Heck yes! Every time one of our Influencer friends bring other influencers on stage or any of this book's three authors on stage, their rooms double or triple in size quite rapidly.

Now, if you bring up a Hollywood celebrity, like Paris Hilton, WHOA! Your room will grow exponentially with the alerts their followers will get every time they speak.

Try it! It's Super Fun to watch your room grow and grow!

CHAPTER 16:
COMMUNITY GUIDELINES

Clubhouse was created as a free space for authentic conversation and expression. Users are expected to have fun while learning and adding value to others around the world.

Users are also expected to demonstrate respect for all community members. Hence, community guidelines are needed to ensure Clubhouse remains free of any attempt to silence members' voices.

To foster meaningful and genuine connections and remain on the platform, you must adhere to the guidelines.

Guidelines To Follow:

Moderators:

Moderators are speakers with the unique power to add or remove other speakers. They guide conversations and direct tone and flow.

The best moderators always:

- Place great emphasis on choosing the right speakers and include diverse people, personalities, and perspectives.

- Actively manage conversations by balancing those who like to talk with more reserved members who may have to be encouraged to speak.

Speakers:

Speakers are members of the audience who are given the privilege to talk to the room. Speakers who are invited by the moderator should always:

- Be prepared to share the stage. This means there could be multiple speakers taking turners to talk. This adds depth to conversations and brings in diverse voices.

- Know when it's best to mute and unmute the mic. It's generally good to mute the mic when you're not speaking, but you don't need to stay muted for the entire conversation - even if you're not talking.

- Periodically unmuting to laugh at a joke, acknowledge the speaker, or just being present in "hangout" style conversations is perfectly acceptable.

Listener:
When you join a room, you're automatically placed in the audience on mute. This makes you a listener. Feel free to just relax and enjoy the conversation.

- Don't feel pressured to participate. Even if you are asked to speak, you're free to decline.

- Remember always to use the "raise hand" if you wish to speak. You will be acknowledged by the moderator and brought to the stage when applicable.

- You can discover more about the people in the room by tapping on their profiles. This is an excellent way to find new people to follow.

- You can split your attention. Feel free to engage in other activities while you listen.

- If you see a friend in the room and want to chat, tap their profile image, and ask them to start a new room together. It's totally cool.

- Exit and enter as you please. You can drop in and out of rooms as you see fit. Don't worry, you won't set off any alerts or offend anyone.

CHAPTER 17:
CLUBHOUSE RULES

Refusal to abide by the rules can result in your removal from the community. Banished. Forever. So be careful.

- Use your real name and identity
- Be at least 18 years of age or older if required by your country.
- Do not engage in abuse, bullying, or harassment of individuals or groups of people.
- Do not discriminate against, engage in hateful conduct directed at, or threaten violence or harm against any persona or groups of people.
- Do not share, threaten to share, or incentivize the sharing of other people's private information without their permission.

- Do not transcribe, record, or reproduce information you receive in Clubhouse without permission.
- Do not engage in conversations or upload content that violates ant intellectual property or other proprietary rights.
- Do not spread false information or spam or artificially amplify or suppress information.
- Do not share or promote information that is intended or likely to cause harm to an individual or groups of people.
- Do not use the service for the purpose of conducting any unauthorized or illegal activities.

CHAPTER 18:
HOW TO REPORT AN
INCIDENT ON CLUBHOUSE

Clubhouse temporarily records the audio in a room while it is live. When a user reports a Trust and Safety violation while the room is active, they keep the audio-only for the purpose of investigation and then delete the temporary audio recording when the room ends.

Audio from audience members and muted speakers is never to be recorded by people in the audience. But don't believe that people aren't nefariously recording. So choose your words wisely and carefully. You're still on a public app.

You can report an incident in two ways:
- Real-time: From inside a room, click on the user you wish to report. A profile half-sheet will pop

up. Tap the three horizontal dots at the top right and then click on "Report an incident." Making a report from inside a room will prompt Clubhouse to retain the temporary audio recording for the purpose of investigation.

- Report a past incident: To make a report after the room has ended, go to your user profile and tap the gear icon at the top right. The tap on "Report an incident." Unfortunately, when you report an incident from your profile, Clubhouse won't have access to the room's temporary audio to support the investigation.

You don't have to fear reporting incidences as:
- Your identity is kept confidential
- The need for and type of disciplinary action is determined on a case-by-case basis.
- Clubhouse seeks to be fair, consistent, and responsive in addressing incidents.
- Intentional, false reports of violations will be treated as a violation of the rules.
- Any attempt to retaliate against members who participate in reporting or investigations is treated as a violation.

CHAPTER 19:
YOUR SAFETY

What if someone hasn't violated the rules, but you still don't want to interact with them?

You're in luck! Here are some tools that you can use.

Moderators:
You have the power to accept or reject speakers. If you want to invite someone to speak, tap on their profile image, and choose "Invite to speak." If someone you would rather not talk to indicates such a need, you can decline.

You can temporarily mute a speaker or move them back into the audience. To mute someone, tap on their profile photo to open the half-sheet and then tap the mute button to the right of their profile photo. To move them back into the audience, tap on their profile picture to open the half-sheet, and choose "Move to Audience."

All members

You can unfollow a member at any time. To do this, go to the user's profile and tap on the button that says "Following" to unselect it. The member won't be notified, and you won't receive any notifications about their activities.

Block. You can block any user at any time. To do this, go to their profile, click the three vertical dots in the top right and choose "Block."

Shared block lists. If many people in your network block a member, you will see a "!" icon on their user profile. This is intended to help you make decisions about who to follow or bring up to the stage.

Clubhouse Court - Where the cat is the judge

Clubhouse Court is for Clubhouse members who cannot settle petty disputes via subtweets, subclubs, or the Clubhouse Parking Lot.

Yup. You'll definitely need this resource if you're going to spend any amount of time on Clubhouse.

Here is the link to learn more about Clubhouse Court - https://clubhousecourt.com

This site will answer questions like:
- Who uses Clubhouse court?
- What if I can't afford an attorney?
- And the all-important question about Clubhouse Court, "Is this for real?"

CHAPTER 20:
10 ROLES YOU CAN PLAY ON CLUBHOUSE

Clubhouse opens up unique opportunities for members to create relevant roles that add value to the platform. Here are 10 personas you can monetize on Clubhouse:

1. Moderator

In each Clubhouse room, you'll find speakers, listeners, and moderators. The moderator is the person to start conversations and has the privilege of choosing other listeners, known as audience members on the app, to speak. Therefore, the moderator is essential to the smooth flow of a room. You can offer your services as a paid moderator on Clubhouse. We foresee this service being in high demand, especially when the app goes mainstream. (Hit us up if you want to get on the waitlist for the CH Moderator certification)

2. Bio Writer

Having a bio that stands out on Clubhouse is very important, but many people are uncomfortable writing their own bio. Some may find it difficult to brag about themselves, so bio writers will also be in high demand on Clubhouse. Bio writers must understand the importance of using the first three lines of the bio efficiently. Additionally, they should ask clients for calls-to-action (CTAs), such as a website link or a database to add leads. Client accomplishments should also be added to the bio. If you see yourself as a bio writer, browse Clubhouse and identify great bios to use as templates and inspiration.

3. Speaker

Before the pandemic, speaking at events was very profitable. In fact, Angie, Alicia and Coach Deb all spoke at events nationally and internationally, and either got paid to speak or they sold their products and services from these stages. Then the pandemic struck, and fortunately, Clubhouse was launched at a time when all stages were shut down. Now professional speakers have the opportunity to present to an audience using the Clubhouse app. Physical stages have moved to the audio stages of Clubhouse, and the best speakers are still monetizing the opportunity and enjoying their craft while on their sofa in pajamas. If you're a professional speaker, you can monetize

Clubhouse by taking your speeches to the app and still having your CTAs (call-to-actions) to sell your programs.

4. Networker

Room hosts on Clubhouse always want to ensure that their rooms are well attended, so if you can join a room and PING a good number of your friends to join as well, you will be well on your way to being a Clubhouse networker. Already, there are room owners who are reaching out to those with a large following and offering them the opportunity to be paid for consistently joining their rooms and pinging a large quantity of friends once inside.

5. Coach

Coaches can teach people how to use Clubhouse, become a better speaker or moderator, and leverage the app for business growth.

6. Room Note Taker

Recording rooms on Clubhouse is frowned upon as of right now and may get you banned from the app. However, this rule may be changing in the near future with parameters and expectations. For the latest updates, check out http://clubhouseconversations.com to hear any news on recording, as well how to go about recording your own rooms in the proper way. In the meantime, you could offer to be a room note taker and provide transcripts of conversations to clients.

7. Connector

Offer services to connect Clubhouse users with those of similar interests. You can connect them in Clubhouse as well as their Instagram and Twitter accounts.

8. Club Admin

Once the platform grows, people will need professional Club Administrators who can manage their clubs for them.

9. Clubhouse Manager (much like a Social Media Manager)

Users may hire you to promote their clubs and rooms across social media so more people get notified and join when your room or club goes live.

10. Room Host

Some users will schedule events for rooms they plan to moderate, however sometimes they may be unable to attend each time the room goes live. Offer to host the rooms for them in their absence.

CHAPTER 21:
BEST PRACTICES ON CLUBHOUSE WITH JEREMIAH OWYANG

When Jeremiah Owyang sent me an invite to download the beta version of Clubhouse App in August, 2020, I'm a little embarrassed to say we had to reschedule a few times because of how busy I was that month.

But in retrospect, it was probably good, because once I downloaded the Clubhouse App, I've never been away from it for very long.

Jeremiah scheduled what's called an onboarding session to Clubhouse, which is where the person who extends the invite to join Clubhouse brings you into a room to welcome you and show you around the app so you'll be successful in using the app, and respect the culture and etiquette of the community, and learn the lingo.

Since I was joining while the app was still in Beta... perhaps still in Alpha... he also showed me how to snap screenshots and report any bugs to the founders and developers of the App, so we could make the app a better place before it was released to the public later on in the year, in October, 2020.

Here are a few things he shared with me during this onboarding process, in the room in Clubhouse.

Jeremiah Owyang, Tech Analyst @Jowyang Shares Best Practices On Clubhouse:

1. For the first five days you've joined the app, you will have the "party popper icon" on your profile, use it to your advantage as people will want to welcome you, and bring you on stage.

2. It's encouraged to bounce around rooms, you don't need to stay "bye" in a group setting. Just hit the "leave quietly" button at the bottom when you're ready to bounce.

3. When on stage, stay on mute unless you're seeking to speak. Then flash your mic button a

few times quickly, to get the attention of the room's host or moderator.

4. Culture continues to evolve, it started out as mostly tech investors and founders, shifted to media and entertainment industry, and now it's going mainstream.

5. Don't be surprised if a (mega) celeb jumps in your room; I'd suggest now is the time to fan boy/girl them or they will leave.

6. Assume everything is on the record. People say "it's a safe space" but a few conversations were unknowingly recorded and published in mainstream media, embarrassing the speakers. Own your words.

7. Men are encouraged to be mindful to let women speak, and not talk over women, as we've noticed that's what the tendency is.

There were a few more tips Jeremiah shared with me on my first day in Clubhouse, but I pause at this last tip, because I remember smiling, thinking, "Oh good luck with this once the digital marketing big-wigs come aboard."

And sure enough... 6 months later, I heard women "asking if they could speak" while men talked loudly over them, so they'd be heard. Ahhhh if only every guy got an onboarding session with my friend Jeremiah

Owyang, someone who always, always, always paused if he heard a woman begin to speak, to which he'd always respond, "Go ahead" or "You First" sharing how he "really wants to hear what you have to share."

Such a gentleman. And such respect he gives to all voices.

I wonder how long Clubhouse will be a respectful place, where we each listen to one another, and let each other take a turn to speak, instead of trying to hog the stage, or argue with one another when our opinions differ from each other.

In a solid attempt to onboard each person I extended an invitation to over the months, one day I went LIVE on YouTube in order to share an onboarding session that all my friends and clients could watch and learn how to use Clubhouse best, because I knew one day, the app would spread like wildfire, and if people didn't have that same experience that I had when Jeremiah patiently passed on the torch, Clubhouse would turn into mayhem.

So, in order to continue paying it forward and have onboarding sessions with each person I shared an invite to, I had a unique experience to onboard one amazing person who wrote down everything I said during her onboarding session, in an attempt to pass on Jeremiah's best practices, and then she turned it into a post on Facebook.

When I read that post, I thought - this is fantastic! I've got to ask her to include this in my book. And then as we met and had more conversations in Clubhouse I realized... she needs more than a chapter in the Clubhouse Book... she needed to join me and help me write this book - as a collaborative effort.

And now... you know the rest of the story... of how Clubhouse Guidebook was born, and became the first book published on Clubhouse. Although getting it to market as quickly as we did was largely thanks to my other co-author, Alicia Lyttle, who always knew how to make this entire book writing fast and easy.

Thanks Ladies!

And Thanks Jeremiah!

Now, to see how the baton of onboarding was passed, from Jeremiah to CoachDeb and then from CoachDeb to Angie Norris... read on to hear what Angie Norris learned from the onboarding session and her subsequent 12 hours on Clubhouse... and please... pay it forward and do the same as you invite your friends and clients on to join Clubhouse, so the community will grow into an incredible place.

CHAPTER 22:
20 THINGS I LEARNED IN MY FIRST 12 HOURS ON CLUBHOUSE:

---

1.   **Apple IOS users only** (for now...Android coming soon)

It is no surprise that an app that was funded by Silicon Valley's best-known venture capital firms would launch an Apple IOS app first. Once they progress out of beta, it won't be long before the Clubhouse app is available to all Android users. For now, you must have an iPhone or iPad to download the app.

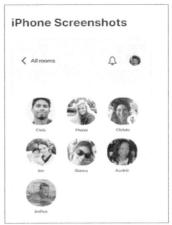

2. You must sign up via the "official" Clubhouse app

Aside from news articles and blog posts, Clubhouse has yet to have its own website so users can find information about this undercover app. For now, you can only access the app via your Apple app store, but beware, there are other Clubhouse apps that are not what you are looking for.

The app has a black and white thumbnail with a groovy, smiling Bob Marley inspired gentleman holding an electric guitar. If you downloaded a faux app, and you were immediately able to get right in, chances are, it is the wrong app.

3. Be sure to secure your username

Usernames are like gold currency in today's social world. So those who take advantage of "First Mover's Advantage" will be the ones who win when it comes to securing your coveted usernames. When I search "Angie Norris" on Google, I'm always amazed at how many hundreds of fellow Angie Norrises there are out there.

Hey Ladies! When it comes to social profiles, I strive to be the first to secure a username of @angienorris and have fallen short of this many times. I've learned my lesson and have become an early adopter of all things new and exciting on platforms to get registered quickly and secure a memorable username. Luckily, I joined Clubhouse during beta back when the app was relatively unknown to many and was able to snag @angienorris as my username.

Don't delay; you can do it within a few minutes of downloading the app, even before you are actually invited to join the Clubhouse party.

4.   The app is invite-only, and you must find someone who will invite you

This may seem hard to believe, but it is very much true. The intention and initial premise behind the app is to have an app that has like-minded people. Think about it, if you had your own club, wouldn't you want it to be exclusive to those you know and trust? I know I would. Therefore, they have committed to an invite-only style of access, and you must find someone already on the Clubhouse app who will give you an invite.

6:29

🌟 We've reserved **@angienorris** for you, and we'll text you as soon as your account is ready!

To learn more about Clubhouse you can read our blog post. Thank you! 🙏

Got your invite text? Sign in →

5. Invitations to Clubhouse are like having an invite to the Grammys

I'm not sure who it is more painful for: the giver or the receiver. You only get an invite to give sparingly, and when I joined, I only got one invite. Don't they understand that I have a ton of people I want to get in with me? I feel like I am headed to the Grammys (in my dreams, of course), and I only have one ticket to give. Who is going to be that lucky person?

As soon as you announce that you've joined Clubhouse, your list of friends, family, and acquaintances will start to grow as people reach out wanting your only invite.

6. Word on the street is that you only get one invite for your first full week on Clubhouse

My sources have confirmed that the majority of Clubhouse users will only receive one invite to give within the first seven days of being on Clubhouse. Come again?

This causes some complex decision making when you have potentially hundreds asking you for your golden ticket.

149

But not to fret, you will get more after your first week on Clubhouse. I chose the first person who asked me from my close entrepreneur friends.

My advice is to be strategic and choose wisely.

7. Getting more invites is based on your Clubhouse activity

Sure, you can be a fly on the wall in the club and enjoy my beloved pastime of being a people watcher, but Clubhouse rewards you for taking action and stepping up. By joining in on the conversation, speaking on stage, and moderating rooms, you'll be granted the privilege of inviting more people to join you as soon as seven days from when you joined.

8. Are you really able to let your friends skip the line into the club?

I'm not going to hold back, I've done my share of club-hopping in my years, and nothing felt better than letting your friends skip the line into the club as VIPs.

Close your eyes and imagine talking to the bouncer at a high-end club who is sternly guarding the velvet rope barricading the pathway of you and your friends from the entrance to the club. You ask the bouncer if he can let you guys in, and he reluctantly obliges because you have been in the VIP room before, but he has to keep up his stern demeanor. This is how it feels when a notification pops up inside your Clubhouse dashboard that states someone you know "is on the waitlist to join Clubhouse.

You will get credit on their profile for adding them without using up an invite. Let them in?" You can say yes; "Let them in!" or no; "Ignore," but this back-door method can be a pleasant surprise while you are using the app.

Note that you have no control over this method, and the friends who pop up to let in seem random. I was able to get in a few friends within my first few hours because I had their cell phone numbers in my phone.

9.   **The app will always showcase who invites you**

Another clever thing the Clubhouse Founders did was to show everyone who invited you to Clubhouse…forever. This raises the bar as to why it is vital to invite only those with whom you are acquainted. Your profile photo will be tagged to all the people you invite or let in for as long as they are on Clubhouse.

The upside is the "power of proximity" if you invited someone of influence. That influencer's followers will be curious to know who the lucky person was to invite this authority figure into the club. They will check out their bio and see your beautiful face proudly stamped on the invitee's profile.

10. Bar fights can also happen in the digital space

I love the bar and club similes because it has the same feeling. I'm a lady, and of course, I've never gotten into a bar fight (that I remember), but I have had guy friends who did. They got kicked out of the bar or party, and because we were with them, so did we.

As I mentioned earlier, when you invite someone to Clubhouse, your name is listed on their bio as the person who invited them. What is interesting about the rooms and conversations I have listened to in my first 12 hours ranged from super spiritual to super political to super social, and of course, I found a few rooms that are in my wheelhouse of entrepreneurship. Some of the rooms that had taboo topics though evoked some heated conversations. One moderator blocked a speaker and said he would block the person who invited that speaker to join Clubhouse.

The moral of the story is to ensure the person you are inviting is not someone who is going to use some fighting words or press their beliefs onto people who don't want to listen. Don't let this deter you, though; as I started following like-minded people, the rooms with the agenda-driven topics showed up less, and my favorite topics showed up more.

11.   Once someone invites you, the Clubhouse etiquette is for that person to "onboard" you and give you the low down

There is no better feeling than a welcome party. When you finally have redeemed your invite to Clubhouse, you are immediately greeted with a room that has your name all over it, literally. It will say "🎊 Welcome

<first name>" and immediately the person who invited you will get a notification that you have joined and there is a room waiting there ready to welcome you to the party.

The person who invited me was Deb Cole, and I was happily greeted by Deb inside the "🎉 Welcome Angie" room. She gave me the rundown of all things Clubhouse and made me feel comfortable with what I was about to embark on.

I hope you get this VIP treatment when you join, but a tip to ensure you do is when you finally get into Clubhouse, don't leave the main screen for at least 5 minutes. The few people I was able to get in within my first 12 hours included some who didn't get to enjoy their welcome party.

On the flip side, if you invited someone but are not actively on the app when they join, not to worry. The welcome party room for that person will alert all of their

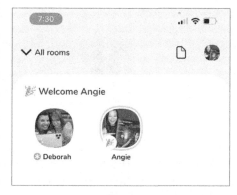

contacts who are active and others will be there to greet them. But be sure to do your due diligence and reach out to them to ensure they were onboarded properly and received all of the information to set them up for

Clubhouse success. If, for some reason, you weren't able to greet them or you are someone who didn't get onboarded in this fashion, you can watch my onboarding video when @CoachDeb welcomed me into Clubhouse at http://clubhouseonboardvideo.com to see how it is done.

12. The first week, you get a party popper badge indicating you are new

When you finally get to enjoy the party inside of Clubhouse, you will notice a party popper emoji at the bottom left of your profile photo. This alerts other users that you are within seven days of joining Clubhouse. You will get grace for accidentally breaking any rules and have lots of people help you get

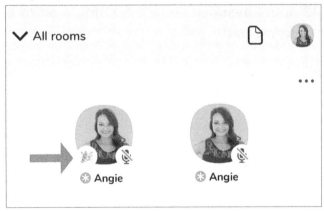

acquainted with the platform. Enjoy the party popper badge while you can; your first week on Clubhouse will go surprisingly fast.

13. Your initial room options on Clubhouse will change drastically as you go

Don't make a judgment on the "type" of audience and room choices you see when you first join Clubhouse because it will change over time. For example, look at Facebook, which started with college kids as the primary audience and now there are more people over the age of 50 than all other age groups.

When I first came into the Clubhouse hallway, the people, as well as the room topics, were not necessarily in my wheelhouse. As I started to follow my entrepreneur friends, influencers I admire, and business besties, I noticed a shift in the rooms, topics, and people who were suggested to me. So keep in mind that Clubhouse will definitely change over time and as the user-base increases from thousands to millions, the possibilities are endless.

14. You can join any public rooms

The power of Clubhouse is that you can join rooms where there are potentially hundreds of people you would not otherwise reach. When I see Grant Cardone, Justine Bateman, Gary Vaynerchuk, Oprah and investors from Shark Tank moderating a room, I immediately get star struck and want to know what they are saying. Now with Clubhouse, you can, by joining any public room that is currently in session. Be a fly on the wall to conversations you wouldn't otherwise hear. Sometimes, you may even get a chance to ask them a question or speak along-side them. Better yet, they may even follow you!

15.   You have to be invited to "speak on stage" and given speaking privileges

When you join a public room that you didn't start, you'll immediately be placed in the audience. However, you may be invited to speak on stage which gives you speaking rights.

There are a few ways for this to happen. The first way is if the event organizer added you as a guest on the event invite in which case, when you enter the room, you'll immediately be placed on stage.

The second way is for you to be in the room's audience and be invited up on stage proactively by a moderator. The third way is for you to raise your hand while sitting in the audience, and your request is granted. Also note that rooms with advanced moderators will move you back to the audience after you speak which is common practice especially in large rooms.

16.   You can start your own rooms

What is great about Clubhouse is that you can immediately start your own rooms. All you do is click the button at the bottom that says "+ Start a room", add a topic by clicking "+ Add a Topic" and then select what type of room you would like to start.

The choices are "Open" which is open to anyone, "Social" which is only open to those you follow, or "Closed" which is only open to those you choose.

Once you have selected the room type, then click "🎉 Let's Go" and your room will immediately begin.

To end a room, you will click the three dots on the top right of the room and select "End Room" to close out the room.

17. There is no limit to how many rooms you run or how long your rooms last

Do you love hosting parties? Well, you are certainly going to love hosting your very own Clubhouse rooms. There is no limit to how many you run, whether it is one a week or 20 a day. You can run them for a concise period or for hours, days, and even weeks. As soon as you enter the Clubhouse experience, you'll immediately be granted privileges to open up and host your own room.

18. If you love live events, then you will love Clubhouse

I believe that true connection happens when you get to have conversations. What better than to meet people at live, in-person events. However, if the world is facing circumstances that hinder the ability to host or attend in-person events, you may not get the opportunity to attend summits, masterminds, presentations, or conferences. Because we have a yearning for human interaction, especially during a pandemic, Clubhouse has been the brand-new way to satisfy that need for deeper conversations that you don't get using traditional social media platforms.

I often compare Clubhouse to a conference in many ways. There are large rooms with prominent, influential speakers where you are just a listener. There are breakrooms where you get to interact. There are hallways where you get to peruse all of the available

meeting rooms and presentations. There are side conversations at the coffee station or breakfast bar. This is exactly how it feels on Clubhouse and I have to say, that I love it.

19. The magic is in the conversations

Purposeful conversation is where the true magic lies. When you meet people for the first time, and have a genuine, passion-driven chat, you will find value in the other person. True connection happens during meaningful conversation and Clubhouse has made it extremely easy for you to do this. You can raise your hand to speak if you are an audience member or if you are moderating your own room, you can guide the topic of conversation.

Either way if you choose to conversate, it is inevitable that you will find the magic of connecting with like-minded individuals through powerful conversation

20. The sessions are NOT recorded, which causes serious FOMO

Although they say nothing is allowed to be recorded, at least for the time being, always be cognizant and speak with the premise that someone "may' be recording. Because the sessions are not recorded, means you have to be there or be square. Those who are not live on the app at the time of the sessions, will not know what truly was said in those rooms. This causes many to have a serious case of FOMO, "fear of missing out" and increases the desire for people to show up and stay indefinitely on the app.

CHAPTER 23:
CLUBHOUSE IS ONLY LIMITED BY OUR IMAGINATION

One of the most viral events on the internet for 2020 was the production of 'The Lion King' on Clubhouse.

Hailed as the most imaginative musical play on the web, it debuted live on December 25 and treated users to an unforgettable experience of a live rendition of the beloved musical.

The 40-member cast included award-winning actor Myles Grier who played Simba along with Mir Harris, embodying the voice of Nala. Other notable cast members were actress and producer Gina Belafonte, Dr. Victor, Minh Do, Shannon Yang, and Felicia

Braithwaite. Live instrumentation, a choir and PTR (pull to refresh) imagery that matched each scene in the show completed the production.

According to Director and executive producer Noelle Chestnut Whitmore, the show's idea was concocted while in a Clubhouse room with Bomani X and Myles Grier where she recognized that Chris "Boogie" Glover, another Clubhouse member, had a distinct voice and would play Mufasa quite well. The idea blossomed, cemented in the goal of spreading joy to people through such events.

Whitmore certainly didn't expect the response the show received. The Clubhouse room for 'The Lion King' musical was so packed that users were left complaining that they couldn't get in. Social media was abuzz with the hashtag #TheLionKingCH trending throughout the day on Twitter.

The success of the show has encouraged Whitmore to expand her reach and leave more indelible impressions on the app. We can't wait to see and talk about what's next.

CHAPTER 24:
THE ROOM WHERE IT HAPPENS

We were in Grant Cardone's room the other night, where a movie deal was born!

Creator of the hit TV series Undercover Billionaire, Aengus James, was in the room, and people began pitching him and asking him all sorts of questions about the TV production business.

Grant Cardone was recently in an episode of Undercover Billionaire, which is a series on The Discovery Channel. So, they discussed a bit more about the show than they

should have, just like in real life when you're chatting it up with your buddies at the pub.

Because no one is supposed to be recording the conversation, you have to be in the room when these discussions occur; otherwise, just like chats in real life at the bar, the dialogue is gone as soon as it's over, and everyone leaves the room.

Suddenly the room turned into a business pitch fest, almost like watching an episode of Shark Tank, except this time, it was like a Radio Show program. One by one, business owners pitched their idea to Grant Cardone, asking him to invest.

Grant has been running rooms that bring in 2,000 or more people in the audience, listening to him talk about real estate investing, movie making, and business growth tips.

Access to Cardone in the past required a hefty conference ticket investment. Now, all you need is to be on Clubhouse, following him or one of his moderators who pings you up on stage, so you can be in the room where big deals are discussed.

Clubhouse is turning up more rooms for business opportunities that's never been seen before in media, and every kind of investor, including Kevin Harrington is showing up in these rooms to see who they can partner up with or invest in who'll help expand their own empire.

We were texting one another on the side, listening as Grant would respond, "Well, what's in it for me?" any time someone came up asking for something, without giving a reason for Grant or any of the other investors in the room, that would benefit them.

PRO TIP for business owners looking to pitch investors:

Just remember, if you're going to pitch a billionaire, be ready to answer the question, "What's in it for THEM?" Don't just ask for something without appealing to how it will benefit the investor.

The moderators of Grant's room were PROS as well. They successfully got people following one another and connecting with the influencers and business investors in the room.

Oh, and I almost forgot to mention, Paris Hilton made an appearance after one of our friends pinged her into the room. She had a quick chat with Grant. They talked about her documentary.

Indeed a moment where everyone got to be a fly on the wall, listening in on a private chat, almost voyeuristic, as two Celebrities connected and had a conversation.

Tyrese Gibson went from popping up in other people's rooms to now where he starts his own room, and talks about the things he does that you won't hear anywhere else.

Early adopters of Clubhouse can see it's a virtual land grab, a free audience builder, and a place to find other influencers making things happen, and collaborating with each other. The ones who understand how to foster joint ventures instead of seeing each other as competition are the ones who'll wind up the winners on Clubhouse, and in real life.

Many are calling Clubhouse "The Virtual Gold Rush", understanding how the ones who are fast action takers, and get in early will get the lion's share of the gold.

Clubhouse is becoming known as the place to be… **in the room… where it happens.**

CHAPTER 25:
21 CLUBHOUSE HACKS
(shhh, keep this between us...)

You've made it! How do you feel? We're hoping you have gained so much insight into the inner workings of Clubhouse that you can't wait to dominate the platform. To further help you jump into rooms and become Clubhouse superstars, we've curated a few hacks that will make you achieve superstardom a little faster. We know...thank us in the Facebook group later. LOL

Hacks to help your friends skip the waiting list and get on Clubhouse NOW:

1. We run an invitation train every Thursday night in our private Facebook group during the holidays and for 5 weeks straight. Now,

we have our group members kick them off, now that they know how it's done.

Here's how it works, so you can do something similar in your own group if you're not part of ours.

First: one of us gives an invite to someone who needs it, they accept and get in and they pass their invitation onto the next person who needs it and so on. Once you join clubhouse you get one invitation, so the key with the train is that when we get someone in - they pay it forward and pass on their invitation to the next person. It works! To date we have an 100% success rate at getting people in. You can join the train by joining our Facebook group at ClubhouseTrain.com

2. Ok, here's another hack, invite people in your phone contacts to join your club. Not only will they get an invitation to join you in your pretty awesome club, but they will also get an invitation to Clubhouse itself! Cool, right? And guess what? You get more friends and clients in your club with this hack. Sweet. We have found that this hack works 80% of the time.

3.   Another way to get friends in is to make sure you have the person that wants an invite is in your contacts before they download the app. Once they download the app, you will get a notification in your "Activity" section that they are waiting to be "Let in." You can allow them access without burning any current invites you may have.

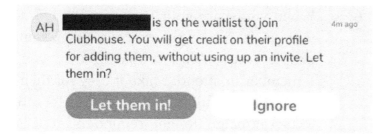

Hacks to grow your room or club

4.   Have some influential friends with a large following? Invite them to your room and bring them on stage! When they moderate or speak, all their fans and those who follow them get a notification of their activities and an invitation to join whichever room they are speaking.

5.   As a host or moderator, do not use the "Start a Room" button at the bottom of your hallway screen to start a room. Instead, schedule all your rooms and club events.

When you do, you will get a link to share on social media or via email easily. If you add other guest speakers when you create the schedule, their fans and yours will receive notifications that your room or club is live one you start it, and they should join via the link sent. Your room will fill much more quickly.

6. When you share your room or club link to your social media pages or via email, some people may worry that they won't remember to attend. Make it easy for them. Ask if they would like to be added to your SMS campaign to get reminders at least thirty minutes before your event goes live. We're sure they will appreciate this. We do!

7. Make sure you connect your Twitter and Instagram accounts to Clubhouse as these are the only two backdoor channels to have people continue conversations off Clubhouse. Having connected to Twitter, use the "Tweet" option to share your room or club details with your fans easily.

8. Copy and paste your room or club link on your social media accounts or in your email so your fans can easily join. Do this more than once leading up to the event in case someone misses it.

9.   When you are creating the title of your room or club event, put an emoji at the beginning of the name and another about, three or four words in. Also, use emojis in the description. Why? Not only because we absolutely love emojis, but when people save your room to their Google calendar and the reminder comes to their email, the emojis will pop in the subject line and help it to stand out among all the other emails they have to sort through. We bet they'll read yours first!

10.   Encourage your fans and friends to add your event to their Google calendars. Remember when you schedule your room you will get a google calendar share link. Before your event they will get an email reminder with a direct link to your event!

11.   When scheduling, add your club as the host and when the event goes live, invite everyone in the room to click the green house button on their screens to follow the club.

12.   When you invite your friends to join a room or club, be proactive in asking them to invite others. Don't just assume that they will invite people without being prompted.

Hacks for your rooms and clubs

13. When you join a club, you are listed in the order in which you enter. So in creating your club, make sure you invite the influencers in your friends list BEFORE you open up the club to the public. In doing so, you guarantee that the people you want to be seen as influencers are at the top, which will help them get more followers, attention, and clicks. Invite strategically!

14. Ensure that your club, and the room you are launching in it, is set to "public" after adding your top ten friends so people will see it in the hallway and join.

15. If you want to be known and invited to other clubs for a particular area of interest (e.g., podcaster, coach, entrepreneur, investor), use the term in your profile a few times. When people search for the particular keyword, your profile will pop up. This helps you to gain authority in that niche.

16. Please don't allow anyone to start a room within your club when it goes live unless you trust them to represent you or your brand.

Hacks for Onboarding

17.   Quickly change your profile image by pressing on your profile picture in the top right-hand corner of your phone for at least five seconds. This will instantly open the photos in your phone gallery. Choose the one you want and voila! All done.

18.   It's easy to spend too much time moderating rooms and not creating content to share. Find other people willing to help you moderate and delegate the responsibilities.

19.   Never miss a Clubhouse notification! Go to your phone Settings, then Notifications. Select "Preview on home screen" to turn it on. Scroll to the bottom to "Show Previews" and choose "Always."

20.   Clubhouse is always adding new components to make your experience unique and memorable. Stay on top of current additions and ways to use the tools by learning from others who frequently use the app (that should include us, of course!).

Hacks for speakers

21.   Put your phone on Do Not Disturb and/or
       Airplane mode so that your phone does not
       ring while you are speaking on Clubhouse.
       Please test the settings on your phone to see
       which mode, or using both, is the best fit for
       your needs.

CHAPTER 26: WILL CLUBHOUSE KILL IN-PERSON CONFERENCES?

The authors weigh-in with a quick chat right before this 1st Edition book comes out...

Conferences provide an opportunity for like-minded people to gather, connect, exchange ideas, and do business.

And it's a lucrative sector.

According to a study by the Oxford Economics and Events Industry Council, the global industry is estimated at $1.1 trillion, with six million international participants generating $38 billion to the sector in 2018.

However, many meetings and conference organizers have had to postpone or cancel events entirely since the beginning of the COVID-19 crisis.

But people still crave networking and exchanging ideas.

So, event organizers have turned to the only remaining safe space for large gatherings - the internet. Plenty of conferences have gone virtual. One virtual event platform reported that its virtual events' business grew by 1000% since the start of the 2020 crisis!

While in-person gatherings will resume eventually, the innovations imagined and birthed during the pandemic, like Clubhouse, are sure to remain.

Why?

Tightly-packed in-person conferences will likely be the last types of events to resume once we're cleared to move freely again. This means that conference organizers must hold on to the tools and apps like Clubhouse to keep their audiences engaged.

Clubhouse has conveniently emerged at a time when people's loneliness and the need to have their voices heard are so overwhelming that they crave as much human interaction as is safely possible.

Unlike regular conferences, where speakers share their messages while the audience nods in approval and takes notes, Clubhouse has opened the stage to all audience members. Everyone now has a say and is free to share with the other members of the room.

According to Coach Deb, "Twitter was the first easy-to-use app to give everyone a voice - where people could now talk back to the speaker and each other WHILE the conference happened."

Clubhouse has built on that tremendously. It is empowering people to use their voices to convey what they mean - literally.

"We won't see in-person conferences again without someone wearing AirPods because they are going to be stepping out of those conference rooms and into the hallways to go on stage in Clubhouse. There, they are free to talk to everyone - including the revered speakers,"

Deborah Cole

She suggests that speakers now find innovative ways of getting their audiences involved or risk losing them entirely to Clubhouse.

Other benefits of moving conferences to Clubhouse are the decreased costs associated with attending one and the increased convenience for speakers.

This, Alicia Lyttle knows all too well.

"In January of 2020, I flew from Jamaica to Malaysia, Atlanta, South Carolina, and Utah - all for speaking engagements. I spent most of the month on planes to speak with different groups of people.

Now, with Clubhouse, I can speak on several stages without leaving my house. My speaking colleagues will understand the euphoria of reaching our audiences on a large scale without having to change our clothes, leave our offices or get on a plane. I didn't even have to put on lipstick!

Alicia Lyttle

I still monetize my services just as an in-person conference. As a speaker, this is the way I prefer to engage with my audience. Of course, there will be a new normal for the seminar industry when face-to-face gatherings resume, but until then, live events will continue to move to Clubhouse."

At in-person conferences, awkward moments can be created when members try to flock to celebrities and speakers. There's no such concern on Clubhouse.

"It's amazing how you can literally share the stage with huge influencers as soon as you get on the platform."

Angie Norris

"That's really powerful considering that if you tried this before Clubhouse, it would take training, time, money, and travel to just be in the same building as them."

Angie, Alicia, and Deb have all shared the stage with powerful influencers like Les Brown, Perry Belcher, Kevin Nations, Fernando Cruz and Rich Schefren, just to name a few.

Other platforms have fought to keep up with holding audiences captive. Everything seems to get in the way - work, family life, emails, and ever-ending messages on Slack. But Clubhouse has managed to cement itself as the cure-all app. It doesn't compete with members' activities as they can be in a Clubhouse room, listening and participating while engaging in other activities like cooking or playing scrabble with the kids.

As for the celebrity pull and FOMO, these are Clubhouse's most captivating features.

Celebrities are flocking to the app, enthralled by the disappearing chats after rooms are closed. With no record of what's being said, the freedom to speak is that much more alluring. FOMO is created because you have to be in the room to experience what's happening. Once you leave the app, you leave the conversation.

Clubhouse has changed the future of conferences. Event organizers must now seriously consider combining in-person with virtual meetups. Now that we've discovered the magic of reaching millions in the comfort of our pajamas, it stands to reason that Clubhouse will continue to revolutionize and grow this sector.

CHAPTER 27:
HOW TO STAY CLUBHOUSE OBSESSED AND AVOID BURNOUT

We'll be straight with you - you will become obsessed with Clubhouse.

Having genuine, quality conversations with people who share your interest or are just really interesting will do that to you. Plus, on Clubhouse, they talk back in real-time. The fact that you have to be in the room as the conversations happen doubles the heartache of leaving a room, so you may find yourself glued to a room for hours, not wanting to miss a word.

But we know you have other activities to attend to (like sleeping), so here are a few tips to help you avoid burnout:

- Bear in mind that Clubhouse is like the radio. You don't have to be staring at the phone screen to participate. You can enter a room, mute yourself, and listen while you engage in other activities. Simply use the raise hand feature when you wish to talk.

- Set a schedule to be on Clubhouse and stick with it. Give yourself specific days or hours to consume information on the app and days off to create content.

- Be like Angie; seek help. Angie is a boss moderator, with a room that runs daily and she can't always be there live. So, Angie created the Mod Squad - a group of trusted members willing to help her moderate the room. They are allowed to choose their days, topics and manage the length and tone of conversations.

- Allow conversations to evolve naturally, so you're not pressured to keep it alive or fight to make it enjoyable.

Use your phone to limit the time you spend on Clubhouse. Here's a really easy-to-use hack to do this.

- On your phone, go to Settings and scroll down to "Screen Time." Click on "Screen Time."
- Next, where you see "App Limits," toggle to turn on.
- Then, under "All Apps and Categories," click on "Social."
- A dropdown menu of your social apps will appear. Scroll through to find Clubhouse.
- Click on "Next."
- Input the number of hours you want to spend on the app per day. Once you go over this limit, you will be locked out of the Clubhouse app for the remainder of the day.

BUT...if you're starting to already get the shakes and other symptoms of withdrawal just by the mere thought of being locked out of Clubhouse for a set period, don't worry.

We have a hack to usurp the app limit. Undo the time limit by going back to "Social Apps" under "All Apps and Categories" and change the number of hours you really want to be on Clubhouse. We won't judge.

And just in case you want to continue feeding your addiction… we'd love to meet you in one of our groups or rooms.

Join us in our Facebook Group at ClubhouseConversions.com

Join us on our blog: ClubhouseConversations.com

And maybe you can be part of the next edition of this Clubhouse Guidebook or get on our Podcast.

Remember: Don't be shy, we promise we won't bite…hard.

Until we meet or connect on Clubhouse, Stay Fabulous!

Aloha,

Deborah Cole,
Alicia Lyttle,
Angie Norris

 @Coach...   ✳ Alicia   ✳ Angie

Thank You So Much For Grabbing Our Book & Reading It to Completion! We're Impressed!

FAQs

---

1. **What is Clubhouse?**
   Clubhouse is an invite-only audio-based app where members can hop into themed rooms and talk to other members.

2. **Is Clubhouse a free app?**
   Yes, but it is only currently available to iPhone users.

3. **Does Clubhouse have a video component?**
   No. The app is 100% voice-based.

4. **Can I record conversations on Clubhouse?**
   No, recording conversations is expressly forbidden. *(However a recent update from the founders indicate Podcasters running their own room can record their room to repurpose it but ONLY if they follow the terms and conditions of getting people's permission if they share something on stage to use their recording.)*

5. **Which celebrities have been spotted on Clubhouse?**

Several celebrities have taken to using the app, some of which are Oprah, Jared Leto, Ashton Kutcher, Drake, Kevin Hart, Chris Rock, Mark Cuban, Terry Crews, Jeffrey Katzenberg, and Tiffany Haddish.

6. **How does the Clubhouse app work?**
Participants are allowed to join rooms where live conversations are taking place. Users can actively participate or just listen in. Recordings are not allowed. Once the room is closed, the conversation is over.

7. **How can I join Clubhouse?**
Since Clubhouse is an invite-only app, you have to wait until someone who is on the app invites you. You may also use the hacks we mentioned above to get an invitation or a "let-in".

8. **How many invites does a Clubhouse member receive?**
All new members are allotted one invite.

9. **Is Clubhouse available on Android?**
No, Clubhouse is currently only available to iPhone users but Android users can use an iPad or iPad mini to download the app and secure their username.

10. **What does PTR mean?** Pull to refresh

11. What is the Stage?
The section in a room where speakers are shown.

12. What is the audience?
The section in a room where non-speakers can be seen.

13. How do you clap on Clubhouse?
Mute and unmute the mic quickly and repeatedly.

14. Who is a moderator?
Rooms are managed by individuals known as moderators. They give audience members permission to speak as well as regulate the tone and length of conversations.

15. Can I schedule a series of talks on Clubhouse?
Definitely! You can add your event or series to the calendar and choose whether you want to make it public or private. Scheduled talks tend to get increased attendance since people have time to plan for them.

16. Can I send messages on Clubhouse?
No, there is no way to DM other members. The only clickable links are your Instagram and Twitter accounts so ensure that they are connected. You can invite members to DM you on your social account.

17. Can I sell on Clubhouse?

While Clubhouse is not primarily for selling, members have found creative ways to introduce their products and services on the platform. Ensure that before you start direct selling, you first offer value and then invite interested members to view your website or sales page. Selling via text messaging has become a hot feature of the platform.

18. Who should I follow?

As you spend time on the App, you will be able to make an informed decision on who you should follow based on your interests. Keep an open mind to learning from new people and follow people who are hosting interesting events. The more people you follow, the more rooms you will see in the hallway.

19. How do I increase my number of followers on Clubhouse?

If you want a bigger audience, the best way to get loyal followers is to have great conversations that offer value. Actively participate in rooms and be respectful and personable.

20. What does "tucking someone in" mean on Clubhouse?

Sometimes conversations on Clubhouse are so interesting that no one wants to leave. They may run so many hours that someone eventually falls asleep in a room. Moderators can move this person back into the audience or out of the room by tapping their profile photo.

RESOURCES

FreeClubhouseBook.com
ClubhouseGuidebook.com
ClubhouseConversations.com
ClubhouseConversions.com

ClubhouseGuide.com (Created as the 1st online guide for Clubhouse written by @Ed one of the first to test out Clubhouse App using Test Flight and needed no invite. Follow Ed Nusbaum on Clubhouse. He's a legit OG
ClubhouseCourt.com
ClubhouseTrain.com
remove.bg
canva.com

ONE LAST FINAL NOTE:

Remember to follow us on Clubhouse:
Deborah Cole @CoachDeb
Alicia Lyttle @AliciaLyttle
Angie Norris @AngieNorris

And to all my friends... who've joined Clubhouse recently & followed me and my clubs...

I appreciate you and each of your contributions you add to this Clubhouse community, and my life.

Once all my marketing friends / social media friends / travel blogging friends and my awesome podcaster friends joined Clubhouse in December, I've been filled with even more joy every time I open the app!

Connecting with some of my dear friends I haven't heard from in over a decade gave me all the warm and fuzzies, like a family reunion.

We've all formed renewed alliances and joint ventures that came together faster than on any other social media channel I've ever been a part of... since the days of MySpace. (Yup, I just said MySpace... maybe I'll try a lil comedy on Clubhouse one day?)

What do you think?

Deborah Cole

CH: @CoachDeb

Special Acknowledgment For Producer: Scott S. Bell

Scott asked me a powerful question back in August 2020, that made this book possible to get into your hands so quickly.

When I was sharing how addicted I was to Clubhouse, and saw it as "The NEXT Big Thing" in Media... Scott asked,

> *"So... is CoachDeb writing the 1st Book*
> *on Clubhouse? Like you did with*
> *Twitter?"*

It was that moment that I secured the domain name ClubhouseBook.com ... and the rest... took care of itself, as you'll read further in this book how this book came to be with my co-authors who helped bring it to you as quickly as we could.

Thanks Scott, for always pushing me to do the things I should, sooner rather than later.

And Thank You for being a wonderful TV Producer for the National TV Show I hosted. I couldn't have produced daily content like that without you!

You Are GOLD my friend.

Deborah Cole

Special Acknowledgments:

We would like to thank our editor, the amazing **Karen Blair**, and our book cover designer, the awesome **Kerry Ann Watson**, and our layout and SEO expert **Giannah Smith**.

We are so grateful for all your hard work in helping us get this book into our reader's hands SO quickly. We could not have done it without each of your amazing talents and work ethic to pitch in any day or time of night to beat the deadlines. We Did It! Thanks to you lovely ladies!

We are also thankful to "**Julie**, The Book **Broad**" and all of your helpful and super funny videos you shared in your book writing bookcamp and on your awesome YouTube Channel: BookLaunchers.TV

We learned so much about getting our book written while we laughed in the process at your humor and incredible tips. Especially when there was "A Jackson Appearance." You and your entire team helped me stick to the writing process over the past 6 months - please thank each of them for me and us.

Alicia Lyttle, Deborah Cole, Angie Norris

From Angie Norris:

At a time when the circumstances of the world seem to be keeping us from real-life interaction, I'm thankful for emerging platforms, like Clubhouse, that provide us with ways to overcome communication barriers.

There is something to be said about opening your heart and meeting new people through deep and vulnerable conversations. You never know when someone who crosses your path will change your life, or you will change theirs.

Entrepreneurs naturally seek deeper associations with people, and our ability to empathize and relate to one another is what makes us uniquely human. The bonds we create are the key to building authentic relationships centered on trust, which is essential to both personal and professional success.
The most extraordinary relationships are the ones you never expected to be in, and it was through cutting-edge tools and technologies that I deepened my strong bond with Alicia Lyttle and Deb Cole.

It is incredible how some people arrive into your life and make such a beautiful impact that you can barely remember what life was like without them.

Cheers to these two female entrepreneurs, who have transformed thousands of lives and lead by example. I look up to you in every way and aspire to model you in all my future days.

Nothing but love to you both! #7FEB

Angie Norris
CH: @AngieNorris

From Alicia Lyttle:

You're reading this dedication to see whose names I'm going to mention and why they were so important to inspiring me to be a part of this amazing book … but guess what, this book is dedicated to you.

So, go ahead and **write your name here**:

_____

And now, you have your name in the dedication of a book!

But, as to not disappoint you completely, I will also share some names of people who have been instrumental in this amazing book.

Of course, this book would not be possible without the collaboration of my girls, Coach Deb Cole @CoachDeb and Angie Norris @AngieNorris! To work with such amazing ladies is truly a treasure!

We hired a few of my students (ladies who had purchased a course from me) who helped us from Jamaica: Kerry Ann Watson, Karen Blair, and Giannah Smith. Thank you for jumping in so quickly to get this book published as the **1st Book on Clubhouse**.

To my sister **Lorette** @LoretteLyttle thanks for always jumping in our Clubhouse room asking us, "When will the book be finished?!"

An all-ladies team? As it turns out, yes. But that doesn't mean this book isn't useful for the guys too. In fact, many of our clients and colleagues have already thanked us for putting this Guidebook together, as it's helped them dive into Clubhouse quickly and skip the learning curve.

Now, you get to dive in and enjoy and make the most out of the hottest new social media app everybody's talking about. Oh, and make sure to follow me on Clubhouse @AliciaLyttle

Alicia Lyttle

CH: @AliciaLyttle

One Last Note Of Appreciation...

This book would not be complete if we didn't pause for a moment and think of all the things and people we neglected as we worked night and day and on vacation to get this book in your hands... Most importantly... Our Guys.

To Jason, Greg and Chris: Thanks to your support, your understanding, and your investment in us.

We couldn't have done this as happily without everything you've done for us, cheering us on, bringing us food and coffee when we were starving and tired; vacuuming, and taking care of the kids; even getting out the shop vac to take care of the house.

Heck, you even helped us "do two things at once" when we needed to be in Clubhouse at the same time we needed to get stuff done in our business.

We Appreciate You… and we promise to make it up to you… perhaps a trip to Jamaica to celebrate with our book production team is in order once this book is published!?

NOTE: This pic was taken during a random, guys busting in our book production zoom meeting on the last Saturday night of book writing… perhaps we neglected them for a wee bit too long, eh? We were all tired, but filled with such joy and excitement about what we were about to share with you… once we hit that PUBLISH button.

THANKS GUYS!

Thank YOU For Reading And Sharing Your Voice To The Clubhouse Guidebook!

Now you can share your voice on our blog - where we'll share all the new info and updates on Clubhouse App as it's constantly changing. Since we believe our readers will have even more cool tips, hacks and secrets on all the creative ways to use Clubhouse, our blog is your chance to contribute to this never-ending book.

Stay connected with us and join the Clubhouse Community on Facebook:
ClubhouseConversions.com

We also have a pile of bonuses for you, now that you've finished the book! Go grab 'em here:
ClubhouseGuidebook.com

Share Your Comments on Our Blog Today:
This is where YOU get to be in our book… online!
ClubhouseConversations.com

Get the most up to date Clubhouse MasterClass Book – FREE For a Limited Time:
FreeClubhouseBook.com

Your Clubhouse Conversations + Connections + Clubs + Notes

Your Clubhouse Conversations / NOTES:

Your Clubhouse CONNECTIONS:

@--

@--

@--

@--

@--

@--

@--

@--

@--

@--

@--

@--

@--

@--

@--

Your Clubhouse CLUBS:

Club Name:

Club Meeting Time:

Your Favorite CLUBS:

Club Name:

Club Meeting Time:

Club Host / Admins:

Club Host's Instagram To Engage With:

Club Host's Twitter To Re-Tweet Favorite Resources:

Club NOTES To Follow Up On:

Clubhouse **INFLUENCERS:**

@--

@--

@--

@--

@--

@--

@--

@--

@--

@--

@--

@--

@--

@--

@--

Clubhouse POWER MODERATORS:

@--

@--

@--

@--

@--

@--

@--

@--

@--

@--

@--

@--

@--

@--

@--

Clubhouse FRIENDS – Intagram + Twitter Handles: Connect Offline + IRL

@--

@--

@--

@--

@--

@--

@--

@--

@--

@--

@--

@--

@--

@--

@--